Standard Grade
Chemi
Revision Notes & Mi Maps

Barry McBride

Published by Scot Smart Publishing Ltd

Copyright: Scot Smart Publishing Ltd

Illustrations by Barry McBride and Tom Heffernan

ISBN 10: 0-9553346-0-8

ISBN 13: 978-0-9553346-0-3

Printed and bound in Scotland

WELCOME
To Standard Grade

CHEMISTRY

Students

This book has been developed to deliver the Standard Grade Chemistry course in such a way as to be enjoyable and easy to read. To get the most from this book it is essential that it is read carefully and at a steady pace to allow yourself time to understand the concepts and theories. Throughout the book there are Top Tips and definitions that must be learned, pay particular attention to these as they will help greatly with your knowledge and understanding. Most importantly work hard, always do your best and **good luck!**

Teachers and Parents

This book has been developed to cover all the learning outcomes as outlined in the SQA arrangement document for Standard Grade Chemistry. It is written in such a way as to be accessible to pupils and deliver the concepts and theories in a "straight to the point" manner using clear and simple language. It is full of helpful hints and proven classroom methods of delivering difficult concepts in a style that the pupils can relate to and understand. This book has been designed to be used both as a classroom aid for the teacher and for a pupil's own personal study. We at Scot Smart Publishing would like to take this opportunity to wish your class or child every success in their studies and upcoming exams and thank you for purchasing our product.

Please feel free to contact us at **www.scotsmartpublishing.co.uk** with any comments or to receive details of any other Scot Smart Publishing products.

Acknowledgements

The author and publishers would like to sincerely thank those who helped in the production of this book especially the two Lesleys, Mary McBride, Cameron Heggie, Dianne Boe, Margaret Sweeten, Michelle Perkins, Sarah Trotter, Alyson Lovie, Gillian Kinloch, Holli and Taelor Coleman.

Plus, special thanks to Bob Nicol and Eddie Keane for their constructive comments.

Orders

Please contact Scot Smart Publishing Ltd, 9 Blair Athol Wynd, Carfin, Motherwell, ML1 4FT.

Web: www.scotsmartpublishing.co.uk

Email: info@scotsmartpublishing.co.uk

Contents

CHEMICAL REACTIONS

TOPIC 1

Chemical reactions happen every second of every day: the burning of petrol in a car engine, the hardening of glue, the rusting of iron. Topic 1 defines what a chemical reaction is and how you can identify them.

Chemical Reactions

Chemical reactions involve the formation of one or more new substances called products.

Word equations are used in chemistry to summarise a reaction. They show the reactants and what new substance(s) are made as a result of the reaction (the products).

Magnesium + Oxygen Magnesium oxide
(REACTANTS)   (PRODUCT)

The Indicators of Reaction

How can you tell if a reaction is actually taking place?
The indicators of reaction listed here is all you need to look out for:

Colour Change   A change in colour indicates that a reaction has taken place. For example frying an egg is a chemical reaction with a colour change, it turns from colourless to white.

Gas Evolved   During a reaction a gas can be given off. This can be shown by bubbles through the solution or by a gas leaving the beaker. For example burning a candle releases a gas (smoke).

Solid Formed   When two solutions mix and a solid is formed this is called a **precipitate**. A precipitate is an insoluble solid formed from two liquids reacting. For example when milk turns very sour a solid is formed.

Energy Change   An energy change usually involves a change in temperature either up or down. For example when a match is lit both heat and light are given off. (See exothermic and endothermic reactions further on)

Energy Changes

During a reaction, energy can be given out or taken in. This means that the temperature will increase or decrease or something will happen like a bright light given out or a loud bang being produced. These types of reactions can be put into two categories.

Exothermic An exothermic reaction is one in which heat (or light) energy is given out to the surroundings.
This means that the temperature will increase.

Endothermic An endothermic reaction is one in which heat energy is taken in from the surroundings.
This means that the temperature will decrease.

Elements

Everything in the world is made from elements. There are over 100 known elements. All the elements we know of so far are in the periodic table.

Elements are substances made up of only one type of atom.

Each element has its own symbol and atomic number.
For example:

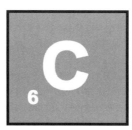

The element shown here is carbon.

The number at the bottom (6) is called the atomic number. Only carbon has this atomic number (the number appears above the symbol in the periodic table).

Not all symbols are as straight forward as carbon. For example

The symbol for lead comes from its Latin name Plumbum. This is why it has the symbol Pb.

Compounds

When elements join together they form compounds.

A compound is formed when two or more elements are chemically joined together.

For example:
When sodium reacts with chlorine the compound sodium chloride is formed.

Sodium + Chlorine   ➡   Sodium chloride
(element) (element)   (compound)

Naming Compounds

Naming compounds is fairly easy if you follow these rules.

RULE 1   If the compound contains only two elements then the name ends in "ide". For example:

Calcium + Oxygen   ➡   Calcium ox**ide**

RULE 2   If the compound contains three or more elements one of which is oxygen then the compound name will end in "ate" or "ite".
For example:

Calcium + Carbon + Oxygen = Calcium Carbon**ate**

Mixtures

A mixture is when two or more substances are mixed but NOT chemically joined.

That means that they have not reacted, for example, a mixture of sand and salt. Mixtures can usually be separated quite easily

Solutions

The following statements must be learned, but don't worry the next TOP TIP! will make this easier.

- A **solvent** is the liquid that the solute dissolves in.

- A **solute** is the solid that dissolves.

- A **solution** is formed when a solute dissolves in a solvent.

- A **concentrated** solution is one in which a lot of solute is dissolved in a solvent.

- A **dilute** solution is one in which a little solute has been dissolved in a solvent.

- A **saturated** solution is one in which no more solute can dissolve.

When learning all the new words associated with solutions it is easy to get confused because they all sound the same.

An everyday and easy example of solutions is when a cup of tea is made. Everyone knows how to make a cup of tea. You make the tea using the tea bag and then add sugar. Easy. If you know how to do this then you know everything you need to know about solutions.

> ### TOP TIP!
> The Tea is the **solvent** (the Liquid).
> So that means that the sugar must be the **solute** (the Solid).
> And together they make the **solution**.
>
> If you remember that the liquid is the **T**, then you remember what the solven**T** is because it is the only word that ends in **T**.

Separation Techniques

Mixtures can usually be separated quite easily using one of the following techniques:

Filtration - Separates an **insoluble** solid from a liquid.

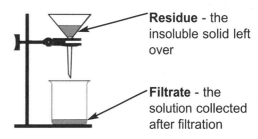

Residue - the insoluble solid left over

Filtrate - the solution collected after filtration

Evaporation - Separates a **soluble** solid from a liquid.

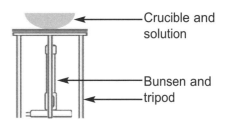

Crucible and solution

Bunsen and tripod

Chromatography - Separates a small mixture of liquids.

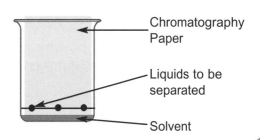

Chromatography Paper

Liquids to be separated

Solvent

TOPIC 2

RATE OF REACTIONS

Chemical reactions can take a few seconds, like an explosion, but some reactions, like the formation of oil, can take millions of years. In Topic 2 we will find out why reactions occur at different rates.

Factors Affecting Rate

There are three factors that affect the rate (speed) of a reaction.

- ⊗ **Temperature**
- ⊗ **Concentration**
- ⊗ **Particle Size**

Temperature

The higher the temperature, the faster the rate of reaction.

The lower the temperature, the slower the rate of reaction.

For example:
If food is kept in the fridge the reactions that cause the food to go off are slowed down allowing the food to last longer.

Concentration

The higher the concentration the faster the reaction.

The lower the concentration the slower the reaction.

For example:
If equal volumes of chalk powder are placed in a beaker of dilute acid and a beaker of concentrated acid the chalk will react much faster in the more concentrated acid.

Particle Size

The smaller the particle size the faster the reaction.

The larger the particle size the slower the reaction.

This is due to surface area. Smaller particles result in a larger surface area.

For example:
A sugar cube dissolves slower than sugar powder. This is because the powder has a small particle size, and therefore a large surface area.

There is a fourth factor that can affect the rate of a reaction.

Catalysts

A catalyst speeds up the rate of a reaction but is not used up in the reaction.

For Example:
In a car exhaust there is a platinum (and other transition metals) catalyst that can change the harmful gases into less harmful gases.

Catalysts also allow reactions to be done at lower temperatures, and therefore less energy is required, which saves a lot of money in industry.

> **TOP TIP!**
> When an experiment is being done and a catalyst is required, if 10g of catalyst is added then 10g of catalyst will still be present after the experiment is finished because they are not used up in the reaction.

There are examples of catalysts in nature.

Enzymes are biological catalysts.

They occur naturally in the body and help with digestion. They are also used in the production of alcohol.

Rate Graphs

In chemistry graphs can be used to follow the course of a reaction. A graph can tell us many things about a reaction. For example:

The graph below shows two similar reactions with chalk and acid, measuring the volume of gas produced over time. One of the reactions is using chalk powder and the other chalk lumps.

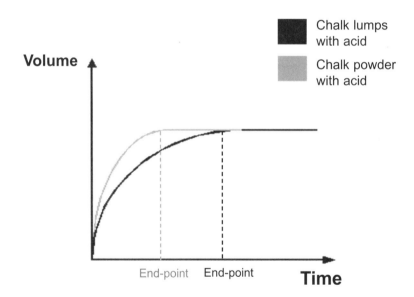

When a reaction is finished (the end-point) the graph goes flat.
It can clearly be seen from the graph that chalk powder reacts faster than chalk lumps because the end-point is reached much faster.

ATOMS & THE PERIODIC TABLE

TOPIC 3

In Topic 1 we learned that there are over 100 elements. In Topic 3 we have to find out why these elements are different from each other and why they are arranged the way they are in the periodic table.

Periodic Table

The periodic table is a table that lists all the elements in a specific order which helps us understand why elements react like they do and what other properties they might have.

For standard grade chemistry there are four main groups of the periodic table that you have to learn. A group is a column of elements in the periodic table. The transition Metals are a block of elements.

Alkali Metals | The alkali metals are a group of very reactive metals. They react with water to produce an alkaline solution. They are stored under oil so that they don't react with any moisture in the air.

Halogens | The halogens are very reactive non-metals.

Noble Gases | The noble gases are very unreactive non-metals.

Transition Metals | The transition metals all have different properties.

Periodic Table Facts

 In the entire periodic table only 2 of the elements are liquids. They are Mercury and Bromine.

 The zigzag line separates metals from non-metals. The metal elements are on the left hand side of the zigzag line and non-metals are on the right.

The Structure Of The Atom

Everything in the world is made of atoms. The structure of the atom is what gives an element it s chemical and physical properties.

Atoms are made up of three smaller particles called:

Electrons Negatively charged particles that spin around the positive centre of the atom in circles called energy levels. (Imagine how the Moon spins around the Earth). Their mass is so small it is nearly zero.

Protons Positively charged particles that are contained in the nucleus of the atom (the centre). They have a mass of 1 amu (atomic mass unit).

Neutrons Neutrons are also contained in the nucleus of the atom but have no charge. They also have a mass of 1 amu.

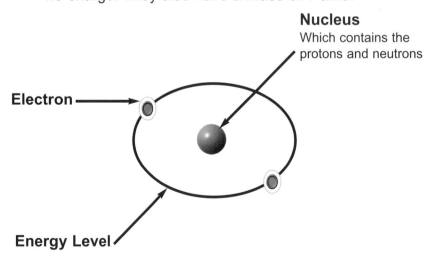

Nucleus
Which contains the protons and neutrons

Electron

Energy Level

The nucleus has a positive charge because it contains all the protons.

Particle	Mass	Charge	Location
Electron	Approx 0	-1	Energy Level
Proton	1 amu	+1	Nucleus
Neutron	1 amu	0	Nucleus

Every atom has no overall charge (neutral), this is because they have the same number of positive protons and negative electrons. These opposite charges cancel each other out making the atom neutral.

Atomic Numbers

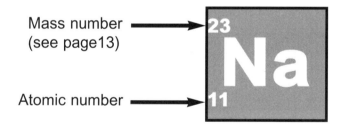

Mass number (see page13)

Atomic number

Each element has its own atomic number.

The atomic number of an element tells you how many protons that element has. For example the element shown here is sodium and has 11 protons. This is written at the bottom left hand side of the symbol.

Because atoms are neutral then it also must have 11 electrons to cancel out the 11 protons.

This information allows us to draw a diagram of a sodium atom showing how the electrons are arranged.

The electron arrangements of all atoms can be found in the data booklet. Sodium for example has the electron arrangement 2,8,1. As you learned previously atoms are made up of energy levels. These energy levels can only hold a certain amount of electrons. The first energy level (the one nearest the nucleus) can hold a maximum of 2 electrons with the others being able to hold up to a maximum of 8 electrons (this is only true for the first 20 elements).

For example: Na 2,8,1

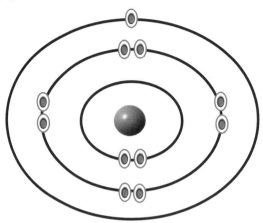

Sodium has 11 electrons so 2 go into the first energy level (the one nearest the nucleus), 8 electrons go in the second energy level which leaves one that must go into the outer energy level.

TOP TIP!
Draw the structure of each atom for the first twenty elements using the electron arrangements in your data booklet.

It is the number of electrons in the outer energy level that gives an element its chemical properties. This is why elements in the same group of the periodic table react in very similar ways. All the alkali metals for example have 1 outer electron. This makes them all very reactive.

Mass Numbers

We can now work out the number of protons and electrons in an atom and draw a diagram of how the electrons are arranged. We must also be able to work out how many neutrons there are in the nucleus of an element.

To do this we must know the mass number of an element.

The mass number is given at the top left of the elements symbol, for example, sodium has a mass number of 23.

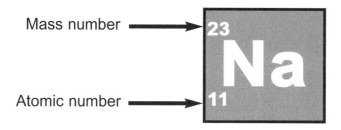

As we worked out earlier the atomic number of sodium is 11. This tells us that sodium has 11 protons and because it is neutral it has 11 electrons.

Sodium has a mass of 23 a.m.u. This can be explained by doing this simple calculation:

Mass of protons   = 11 a.m.u
Mass of electrons   = 0 (electrons have no mass)

Then the number of neutrons must be 12 to give sodium a mass of 23.

TOP TIP!
Remember that electrons have a mass of zero and therefore don't affect the mass of an element.

Here are some more examples:

Element	Mass Number	Protons	Neutrons
Magnesium	24	12	12
Potassium	39	19	20
Carbon	12	6	6

Remember - the number of electrons is equal to the number of protons in an atom.

Isotopes

The mass of the atoms of an element are not always the same. Just as people are all different weights, atoms also have slightly different weights.

Isotopes are atoms with the same atomic number but different mass number.

For example:

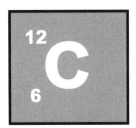 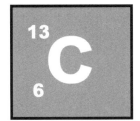

These two carbon atoms are isotopes, they have the same number of protons, however, the number of neutrons are different.

Elements are made up of isotopes so the mass given in the data booklet is called the relative atomic mass (RAM).

It is an average of all the masses of the isotopes of an element. Taking into account the % proportion of each isotope.

TOP TIP!
Remember - The relative atomic mass (RAM) is an average, so it is rarely a whole number.

HOW ATOMS COMBINE

Now that we know what an atom is we now have to learn about how these atoms combine and what holds them together.

Molecules

A molecule is two or more atoms held together by covalent bonds.

For example a molecule of water is H_2O.

It has two hydrogen atoms and one oxygen atom, all held together by covalent bonds.

A molecule is usually made up of non-metals only.

Covalent Bonds

The noble gases are like the pop stars or movie stars of our world. All elements in the periodic table want to be like them in every way. This is why noble gases won't react because they don't want to be changed in any way. They are perfect the way they are. In chemistry terms they are said to be **stable.**

If elements are to be like their heroes they must try to achieve the same electron arrangement as a noble gas, which is a full outer energy level. For example, neon has 8 outer electrons whereas oxygen only has 6 outer electrons, so to become stable like a noble gas, it must gain two electrons from another atom. This is why bonds are formed.

The bonds formed are called Covalent bonds.

A covalent bond is a shared pair of electrons between two non-metals.

The atoms are held together because of the electrostatic force of attraction between the positive nucleus of each atom and the shared pair(s) negatively charged electrons.

This is better illustrated as a diagram:

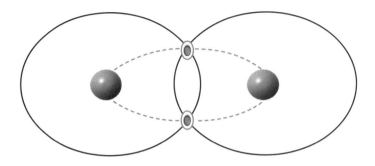

⬤ **Nucleus**

◉ **Electron**

The saying "opposites attract" can be used to describe how a covalent bond works. The positively charged nucleus is attracted to the negatively charged electrons. However the nucleus on the other side is also attracted to them. This creates a "tug-of-war" effect. Both nuclei try to pull the electrons toward themselves creating a strong bond that holds the atoms together. This is shown by the dashed line in the diagram.

The diagram shown is a molecule of hydrogen. Hydrogen has the electron arrangement of 1. So by sharing its electron with that of another atom of hydrogen they both have two outer electrons which gives them the same electron arrangement of the noble gas Helium.

TOP TIP!
Remember the "tug-of-war" description it will help you to describe exactly how a covalent bond holds the atoms together.

Diatomic Molecules

A diatomic molecule is a molecule that contains two atoms.

This means that it exists as pairs rather than single atoms. There are several elements that exist as diatomic molecules. All of which you **must** know.

For example:

Oxygen is a diatomic molecule that is why its formula is O_2.

Again, you must learn all 7 diatomic elements.

For all of the diatomic elements, it is essential that you can draw a diagram of the molecule showing all of the outer electrons. Like the example drawn for hydrogen.

This shows a molecule of fluorine. An atom of fluorine requires 1 electron to become stable therefore it will share 1 electron with another atom of fluorine to form two stable atoms.

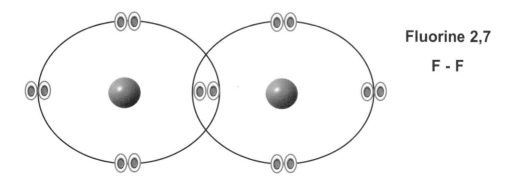

Fluorine 2,7

F - F

Oxygen has the electron arrangement 2,6 and requires 2 electrons to become stable. Because of this it must share two electrons with another oxygen atom. This means that oxygen forms a double covalent bond.

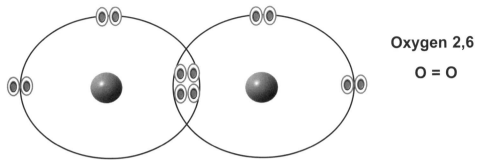

Oxygen 2,6

O = O

There are also some diatomic compounds such as Carbon Monoxide (CO) and Hydrogen Flouride (HF).

TOP TIP!
Draw a diagram showing all the electrons involved for all the diatomic elements. There is usually one in the exam.

To make sure you have drawn the diagrams correctly just count the electrons. Each atom should have eight. Except for hydrogen it should only have 2. If they don't, try it again.

Chemical Formulas

H_2O and CO_2, where do chemists get these formulas from? It is easy if you follow this simple system.

Before we do formula we must learn about a thing called valency. Valency is the number of bonds that an element can form. The valency of an element can be worked out using the data booklet.

The valency is shown below. This means for example, that all the alkali metals have a valency of 1 etc.

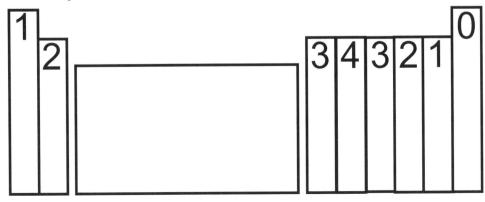

To write a chemical formula it is best to use the **S.V.S.D.F** system.

For example, what is the formula of potassium oxide?

Symbol   K   O

Valency   1   2   (Always use your data booklet for valency)

Swap   2   1

Divide   2   1   (divide by the smallest number)

Formula K_2O

When dividing always use the smallest number. In the case above that is 1 and therefore makes no difference to the formula. If the numbers don't divide into each other for example 2 into 3 then miss this stage out.

For example: aluminium oxide.

Symbol   Al   O

Valency   3   2   (Always use your data booklet for valency)

Swap   2   3

Divide   2   3   (divide by the smallest number)

Formula Al_2O_3

Another example: carbon sulphide.

Symbol   C   S

Valency   4   2   (Always use your data booklet for valency)

Swap   2   4

Divide $\frac{2}{2} = 1$ $\frac{4}{2} = 2$ (divide by the smallest number)

Formula CS_2

Complex formula

For example: calcium nitrate.

Symbol	**Ca**	**NO$_3$**
Valency	2	1
Swap	1	2
Divide	1	2
Formula		$Ca(NO_3)_2$

The valency of group ions can be found on page 4 of the Data Booklet.

The valency is the same as the charge shown in the table.

When a group ion is multiplied, it must be put into brackets as shown.

Shapes of Molecules

Certain molecules have certain shapes. The shapes are caused by the repulsion of electrons that are in the bonds. What this means is that particles of the same charge will move away from each other. Because a covalent bond is made up of electrons then the bonds will move away from each other to create the shapes of the molecules shown.

> ### TOP TIP!
> The diagrams shown here appear regularly in Standard Grade exams and it is essential to learn them. Draw them exactly as they are here, to obtain the marks.

METHANE (CH$_4$) - **Tetrahedral in shape**

All molecules that have a formula like methane will have this shape. For example, CCl$_4$ will also be tetrahedral in shape.

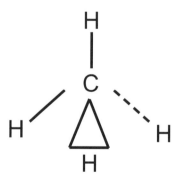

AMMONIA (NH$_3$) - **Pyramidal**

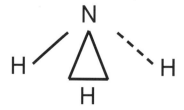

Balanced Equations

A chemical equation is said to be balanced when there are equal amounts of each element on both sides of the equation.

The equation shown below is not balanced because there are two atoms of oxygen on the left, but there is only one atom of oxygen on the right. Atoms can t magically appear and disappear therefore we must balance the equation.

$$Ca \ + \ O_2 \longrightarrow CaO$$

Balancing equations can be difficult so take your time!

Step 1   Check that all the formulas in the equation are correct.

Step 2   Deal with only one element at a time.

For example:
There is one calcium atom on the left, and one calcium atom on the right. Therefore the calcium atoms are balanced.

Step 3   If balancing is required, put the required number in **front** of the substance.

For example:
There are 2 oxygen atoms on the left and 1 on the right, therefore multiply the compound on the right by 2 as shown below:

$$Ca \ + \ O_2 \longrightarrow 2CaO$$

Step 4   Check each element again and repeat step 3 if required

For example:
There are now 2 calcium atoms on the right and only 1 on the left, therefore multiply the calcium on the left by 2 as shown below:

$$2Ca \ + \ O_2 \longrightarrow 2CaO$$

Practice as many of these as you can!

TOPIC 5

FUELS

Fuels are one of the most important substances on earth. They cook your food, heat your home, and keep the cars and trains running. Without fuels the world would be a different place.

A fuel is a substance that burns to release energy.

To put it another way a fuel is a substance that reacts exothermically with oxygen.

Combustion

When a substance burns it reacts with oxygen. This is known as combustion. All combustion reactions are exothermic because they release energy.

For example:

When methane is burned in a bunsen burner, heat energy is given out.

As combustion is the reaction of a fuel with oxygen, then it is obvious that oxygen must be present for combustion to take place. The oxygen required comes from the air.

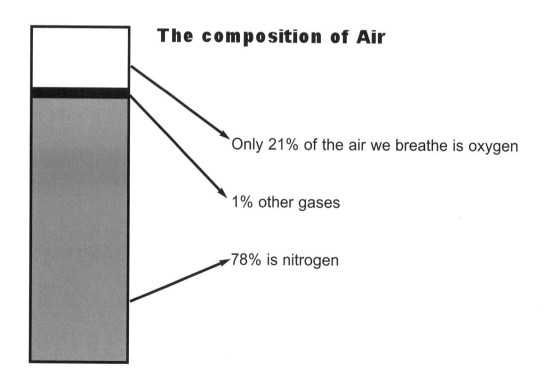

The composition of Air

Only 21% of the air we breathe is oxygen

1% other gases

78% is nitrogen

The test for oxygen in the lab is simple because **oxygen relights a glowing splint**.

For Example:

Test tube of Air

Test tube of Oxygen

Glowing splint
does not relight

Glowing splint
relights

Products Of Combustion

When a compound burns it reacts with oxygen. Because of this we can predict what the products of the reaction will be. The oxygen will combine with each individual element in the compound.

In the example below methane (CH_4) is being burned. The oxygen will combine with the carbon and the hydrogen in the methane molecule to produce carbon dioxide (CO_2) and water (H_2O).

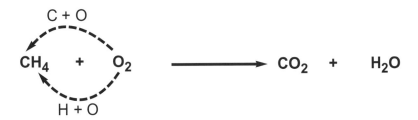

When any hydrocarbon is burned completely, carbon dioxide (CO_2) and water (H_2O) are produced.

To prove this the products of combustion have to be tested. This is done using the following experiment.

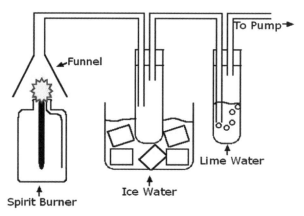

To test for carbon dioxide, lime water is used. If carbon dioxide is present the lime water will turn from colourless to milky white.

If H_2O is produced the water will condense in the ice water test tube. Water boils at $100^O C$ and freezes at $0^O C$.

Fossil Fuels

Coal, oil and gas are known as the fossil fuels. They are incredibly important substances in our modern world as they provide energy for transport, electricity, and heating for homes.

They are called the fossil fuels because they were formed by dead plants and animals kept under pressure for millions of years like fossils.

Coal   Formed from dead plant material and is used by Power Plants to produce electricity for our homes.

Oil   Formed from dead sea creatures and plants. Oil can be treated to produce many substances such as petrol, plastics, diesel and tar.

Gas   Formed alongside both coal and oil, but more usually with oil. Known as Natural Gas, it is used to heat homes.

All 3 fossil fuels are said to be finite, this means that they are running out and cannot be replaced.

Obviously this will have a major impact on our way of life. So scientists are currently developing alternative sources of energy such as wind, solar, and biomass.

Crude Oil

Crude oil is a black sticky substance. However, hidden in it are many different compounds that have essential everyday uses, such as petrol, diesel, lubricating oil, tar and many other substances that play very important roles in our everyday lives.

These compounds are known as:-

HYDROCARBONS

Hydrogen   Carbon

Compounds that contain hydrogen and carbon only.

These hydrocarbons all have different boiling points. This allows us to separate them.

The crude oil found must be converted into these useful products by a process know as fractional distillation.

Fractional Distillation

Fractional distillation is used to separate crude oil into fractions.

A fraction is a group of hydrocarbons with similar boiling points.

Because each fraction has its own boiling point, then if the crude oil is heated, each fraction will boil at different temperatures and leave the crude oil mixture as a gas. This allows them to be collected separately.

This is done in a fractionating column:

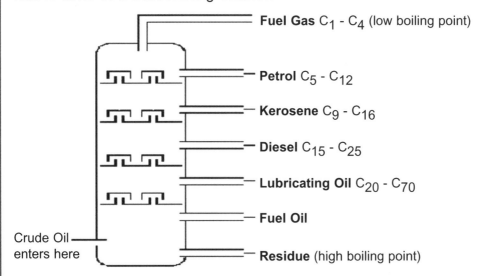

The fractions produced all have different boiling points but they also have different properties such as flammability and viscosity.

Viscosity is a measure of how thick or runny a liquid is.

You can say treacle has a high viscosity because it is very thick.

The change in viscosity and flammability show a pattern. This is best shown in a diagram:

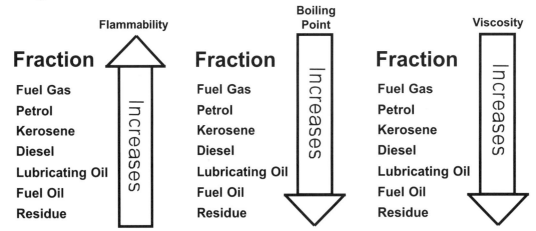

As molecular size increases both boiling point and viscosity increased, however, flammability decreased.

These properties are due to molecular size. The larger the molecule the more forces of attraction there is between the molecules. This makes them thicker', with higher boiling points, and less flammable.

Pollution

Fossil fuels have a major disadvantage as a fuel. They contribute greatly to pollution. Two of the pollution problems that they contribute to are the greenhouse effect and acid rain. These are caused by the gases produced when fossil fuels are burned. Some of the gases that contribute to these problems are:-

 ## Carbon Dioxide

Carbon dioxide is produced on combustion of any hydrocarbon. It contributes to the greenhouse effect which in turn leads to global warming.

 ## Carbon Monoxide

Carbon monoxide is a highly toxic gas produced by incomplete combustion. Incomplete combustion occurs when there is not enough oxygen present to burn the fuel completely which leads to a dirty flame and the production of carbon monoxide.

$$C \;+\; \frac{1}{2}O_2 \longrightarrow CO$$

 ## Sulphur Dioxide

Sulphur is an impurity in fossil fuels. When fossil fuels are burned SO_2 is produced. SO_2 dissolves in water to produce an acid. It contributes to the acid rain problem. Acid rain damages plants and speeds up the corrosion of iron structures and limestone buildings.

 ## Nitrogen Oxides

Nitrogen is a very unreactive gas. However, when a large spark is passed across nitrogen mixed with oxygen, it will break down and form nitrogen oxides. The spark from a spark plug in a petrol engine allows this to happen (diesel engines don't have spark plugs so they don't produce this gas). This gas also contributes to acid rain.

How can pollution be reduced?

Pollution can be reduced in a number of ways. For example:

Lean-Burn Engine

A lean-burn engine increases the amount of air to petrol in a car engine. This reduces the quantity of carbon monoxide produced.

Catalytic Converter

This is a special exhaust system containing platinum. **It converts harmful gases into less harmful gases.**

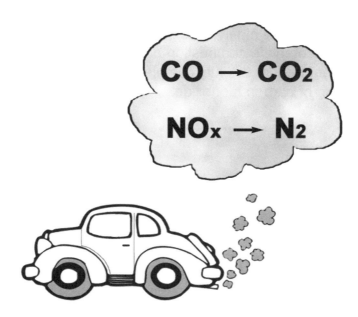

$$CO \rightarrow CO_2$$
$$NO_x \rightarrow N_2$$

Catalytic converters only work with unleaded petrol. This is because the lead in leaded petrol poisons the catalyst.

Using low sulphur petrol can reduce SO_2 in the atmosphere.

HYDROCARBONS

In Topic 5 we found out that Hydrocarbons are compounds made up of carbon and hydrogen only. In Topic 6 we will discover that the Hydrocarbons make up families of compounds called homologous series.

A Homologous series is a family of hydrocarbons with similar chemical properties and can be represented by a general formula.

For example:
Victoria McBride is the oldest member of the McBride family. She has a sister Zoe McBride and a brother Jack McBride. They all belong to the same family, that is why the have the same ending to their name. Although they are all part of the same family they look slightly different and act in slightly different ways.

This is the same as any Homologous series. They are a family with similar names and characteristics, but each member is slightly different.

There are three Homologous series (families) that you have to learn for Standard Grade. They are the **Alkanes, Alkenes**, and the **Cycloalkanes.**

Alkanes

The first homologous series is the ALKANES. All alkanes have the same ending to their names - **ANE.**

The alkanes have many uses:

Methane - (natural gas) cooking, heating

Propane - used in gas cylinders for BBQ etc

Octane - used as petrol for cars

The names, molecular formulas and structural formulas of the first 8 alkanes must be learned.

Name	Molecular Formula	Full Structural Formula
Methane	CH_4	$H - \underset{\underset{H}{\vert}}{\overset{\overset{H}{\vert}}{C}} - H$
Ethane	C_2H_6	$H - \underset{\underset{H}{\vert}}{\overset{\overset{H}{\vert}}{C}} - \underset{\underset{H}{\vert}}{\overset{\overset{H}{\vert}}{C}} - H$
Propane	C_3H_8	$H - \underset{\underset{H}{\vert}}{\overset{\overset{H}{\vert}}{C}} - \underset{\underset{H}{\vert}}{\overset{\overset{H}{\vert}}{C}} - \underset{\underset{H}{\vert}}{\overset{\overset{H}{\vert}}{C}} - H$
Butane	C_4H_{10}	$H - \underset{\underset{H}{\vert}}{\overset{\overset{H}{\vert}}{C}} - \underset{\underset{H}{\vert}}{\overset{\overset{H}{\vert}}{C}} - \underset{\underset{H}{\vert}}{\overset{\overset{H}{\vert}}{C}} - \underset{\underset{H}{\vert}}{\overset{\overset{H}{\vert}}{C}} - H$

TOP TIP!

To make it easy to remember all the alkanes use this little poem. It makes it very easy. Or make up your own.

Monkeys	Methane	CH_4
Eat	Ethane	C_2H_6
Peanut	Propane	C_3H_8
Butter	Butane	C_4H_{10}
Perhaps	Pentane	C_5H_{12}
Harry	Hexane	C_6H_{14}
Heptane	Heptane	C_7H_{16}
Objects	Octane	C_8H_{18}

All homologous series have what is known as a **general formula.**
The general formula allows you to work out the molecular formula of any alkane. The general formula of the alkanes is:

$$C_nH_{2n+2} \text{ (n is the number of carbon atoms)}$$

For example, what is the molecular formula of Pentane?
Using your poem you can work out that Pentane is the fifth alkane and therefore has 5 carbon atoms.

So the molecular formula of pentane is C_5H_{12}

Because **$C5H(2x5+2)$**

Alkenes

The second homologous series is the ALKENES.
All alkene's have the ending -**ENE,** for example Ethene.

They are different from the alkanes because they contain a carbon to carbon double bond which makes them more reactive than the alkanes.

Note that there is no Methene because there must be at least 2 carbon atoms to form a double bond to another carbon.

Name	Molecular Formula	Full Structural Formula
Ethene	C_2H_4	H H | | C = C | | H H
Propene	C_3H_6	H H H | | | C = C — C — H | | H H
Butene	C_4H_8	H H H H | | | | C = C — C — C — H | | | H H H

The alkenes have the general formula:

$$C_nH_{2n}$$

The alkenes are described as being **UNSATURATED**. This means that they have a carbon to carbon double bond. This makes them more reactive than the alkanes because they only have single bonds. The alkanes are said to be saturated because they only contain single bonds.

> **TOP TIP!**
> An easy way to remember which is saturated is **S**cot **S**mart.
> **S**aturated = **S**ingle bonds.

Cycloalkanes

The third homologous series is the CYCLOALKANES.
All Cycloalkane's have the ending -**ANE** but start with **CYCLO**.
For example Cyclopropane.

Name	Molecular Formula	Full Structural Formula
Cyclopropane	C_3H_6	
Cyclobutane	C_4H_8	

The cycloalkanes have the general formula

$$C_nH_{2n}$$

They have the same general formula as the alkenes. The cycloalkanes however, only contain single bonds, which means that they are saturated and not unsaturated like the alkenes.

Isomers

Isomers have the same molecular formula but different structural formulas.

This means that they have they have the same number of carbon and hydrogen atoms but they are arranged differently.

For example:
Cyclopropane is an isomer of propene. They both have the molecular formula of C_3H_6 but the alkenes have a double bond whereas the cycloalkanes don't.

Propene   Cyclopropane

Both have the same number of carbon and hydrogen atoms but they have different structures.

Addition Reactions

Reactions between alkenes and hydrogen or bromine are called addition reactions.

An addition reaction usually involves the addition of a diatomic molecule across the double bond of an alkene.

The reaction to identify an alkene involves an addition reaction. When bromine (which is brown in colour) is added to an alkene it is immediatly decolourised. This doesn't happen with a saturated hydrocarbon like the alkanes or cycloalkanes.

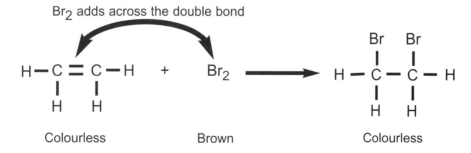

The bromine can be replaced by any diatomic molecule, for example, Hydrogen H_2.

When hydrogen is used it changes an unsaturated molecule into a saturated molecule i.e an alkene into an alkane.

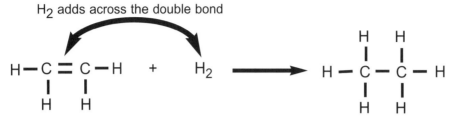

H$_2$ adds across the double bond

This reaction is used to identify alkenes and alkanes. Alkanes have no double bond and therefore will not react with bromine water. Alkenes however react with the bromine by addition. This can be seen because the brown bromine water is decolourised. Addition reactions can also be done with compounds such as H_2O and HBr.

Catalytic Cracking

Fractional distillation produces many products. Some of which are in very high demand i.e. petrol. Products such as residue (tar) are not in as high demand and have a much smaller profit margin. Chemists have came up with a method of breaking large molecules such as tar into smaller much more profitable molecules such as petrol.

Catalytic cracking is the breaking up of long chain hydrocarbons into smaller more profitable molecules using a catalyst. It is done to meet demand and make profit.

The use of the aluminum oxide catalyst allows it to be done at a lower temperature.

The method of catalytic cracking in the lab is done like so:

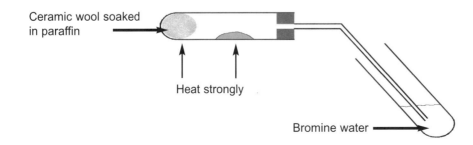

Ceramic wool soaked in paraffin

Heat strongly

Bromine water

When catalytic cracking is performed one of the products is always unsaturated (double bond) this decolourises the bromine water.

Long hydrocarbon $\longrightarrow$ Saturated   +   Unsaturated
Hydrocarbon   Hydrocarbon

The reason that one of the products is unsaturated is because there is not enough hydrogen atoms present to continue with saturation. This is better illustrated with a formula equation.

$$C_8H_{18} \longrightarrow C_5H_{12} + C_3H_6$$

When cracking is performed the octane molecule above is cracked into two smaller molecules one of which has 5 carbon atoms and 12 hydrogen atoms. This leaves 3 carbon atoms and only 6 hydrogen atoms to form the other molecule. This makes it unsaturated.

TOPIC 7

PROPERTIES OF SUBSTANCES

In Topic 4 we learned about covalent bonds. However, in Topic 7 we are going to learn about a new type of bonding called IONIC BONDING.

Conduction

As you should already know metals conduct electricity and non-metals don't conduct electricity (except graphite), but what about compounds?

In topic 4 we learn about covalent bonds, which is a shared pair of electrons between two **non-metals**. But do compounds that are made up of these bonds conduct electricity? The answer is **NO**.

Covalent compounds never conduct electricity.

In topic 7 we are going to learn about a new type of bonding called **IONIC BONDING.**

Ionic compounds are different from covalent compounds because they **never conduct when solid but do conduct when molten or in solution.**

Ionic Bonding

An ionic bond is the electrostatic force of attraction between a metal ion and a non-metal ion.

An ion is a charged particle (like a proton and an electron are charged). Metal ions are positively charged and non-metals form negatively charged particles. These opposite charges are attracted to each other which produces the bond.

Forming Ions

Atoms are trying to become stable. (Look back at Topic 4 for help). To do this they must achieve the same electron arrangement as a noble gas which have full energy levels.

For example:
Magnesium (Mg) has the electron arrangement **2,8,2**

To become stable it must lose its two outer electrons to obtain a full outer energy level.

Atoms are neutral because they have equal numbers of protons and electrons however, when they lose two electrons they are no longer neutral. They change into ions with a two positive charge.

$$\text{Mg} \longrightarrow \text{Mg}^{2+} + 2e^-$$
$$2,8,2 \qquad\qquad 2,8$$

Non-metals form negative ions because they gain electrons to become stable.

$$\text{Cl} + e^- \longrightarrow \text{Cl}^-$$
$$2,8,7 \qquad\qquad 2,8,8$$

When these two charged particles come together they form a ionic bond because the positive magnesium ion is attracted to the negatively charged chlorine ion.

Electrolysis

Electrolysis is the breaking up of an ionic solution using electricity.

The solution that is being broken up must be ionic as covalent compounds don t conduct electricity:

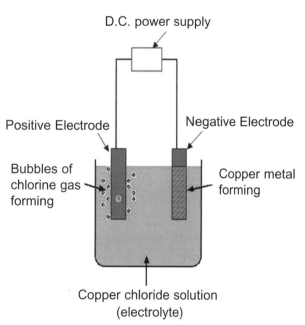

D.C. power supply

Positive Electrode

Negative Electrode

Bubbles of chlorine gas forming

Copper metal forming

Copper chloride solution
(electrolyte)

The copper chloride solution is broken up because when the electricity is passed through the solution, the positive copper ions are attracted to the negative electrode. When the copper ions get to the electrode they pick up two electrons to form copper metal like so:

$$Cu^{2+} + 2e^- \longrightarrow Cu_{(s)}$$

The negatively charged chloride ions are attracted to the positive electrode. When they get there they lose their extra electrons to become chlorine gas like so:

$$2Cl^- \longrightarrow Cl_{2(g)} + 2e^-$$

TOP TIP!
Remember that chlorine is diatomic that is why there are 2 electrons involved and not 1 as you would expect.

During electrolysis a D.C. (direct current) power supply must be used this is because it maintains a constant positive and a constant negative electrode.

Ion Migration

Ion migration works just like electrolysis however, the movement of the ions can be seen.

When the green solution of copper dichromate is electrolysed using a **D.C.** power supply, two different colours can be seen to appear at the electrodes.

Blue copper ions can be seen moving towards the negative electrode and orange dichromate ions can be seen moving towards the positive electrode.

Properties Of:

Ionic Compounds

Ionic compounds form what is known as a lattice structure. This is a regular arrangement of metal and non-metal ions which creates compounds with a **very high melting point** which conduct when molten or in solution but **NEVER** when solid.

This is a diagram of an ionic lattice. It forms a cube like structure. Ionic compounds dissolve in water easily, when they do this their lattice breaks up completely. Therefore they can conduct as the ions are free to move.

> ### TOP TIP!
> If you look very closely at common household salt you will see that the crystals are all cubed shaped. This is because salt is sodium chloride - an ionic compound.

Covalent Compounds

There are two types of covalent compound. Discrete molecular and covalent network.

Discrete covalent molecules all have a very low melting point and boiling point this means that they are either a liquid or a gas at room temperature. Like all covalent compounds they do not conduct electricity in any state.

Covalent network substances, however, **have VERY high melting points and are very hard**. Diamond for example is a covalent network structure and is used in cutting tools for cutting through rock.

Covalent substances are insoluble in water but do dissolve in other covalent solvents such as turpentine.

Bonding Summary

	Ionic Lattice	Covalent Network	Discrete Covalent Molecule
Boiling Point & Melting Point	High	Very High	Low
State at Room Temperature	Solid	Solid	Liquid or Gas
Conduction of Electricity	ONLY when molten or in solution	Never (except Graphite)	Never

ACIDS AND ALKALIS

Acids have a reputation for being nasty chemicals that burn through floors and metal structures with great ease. But did you realise that vinegar is an acid? Topic 8 tackles some of the myths associated with acids and their chemical opposite's alkalis.

Making acids and alkalis

As we learned in Topic 5 when an element is burned, oxygen combines with that element to form an oxide. For example:

Magnesium + Oxygen $\longrightarrow$ **Magnesium oxide**

This is a way in which acids and alkalis can be produced because.

Soluble **metal oxides produce alkalis** when dissolved in water (Base).

Soluble **non-metal oxides produce acids** when dissolved in water.

Acid Rain

Acid rain is a major pollution problem. It is caused by the combustion of fossil fuels that contain sulphur as an impurity. When this sulphur is burned it produces sulphur dioxide which dissolves in rain water to produce acid rain.

Sulphur + Oxygen $\longrightarrow$ **Sulphur dioxide**

Acid rain has many damaging effects on the environment. Some of which are:-

- Erosion of buildings

- Corrosion of metal structures

- Damaging to plant life

- Damaging to animal life (fish)

As we discovered in Topic 5 acid rain can be reduced by using low sulphur petrol and catalytic converters in car exhausts.

pH Scale

The pH scale is a measure of how strong or weak an acid or alkali is. It is a continuous scale from below 0 to above 14.

$$1 \longleftrightarrow 7 \longleftrightarrow 14$$

A pH of **BELOW 7 indicates an acidic solution** (Universal Indicator turns a red or orange colour).

A pH of **ABOVE 7 indicates an alkaline solution** (Universal indicator turns a blue or purple colour).

A pH of **7 is a neutral solution** such as pure water (Universal indicator will stay green).

Acidic Solutions

Acidic solutions have a pH less than 7. This is because they contain more H^+ ions than OH^- ions. H^+ ions are why acids react like they do, and all acidic solutions contain H^+. All acids conduct electricity because they contain ions that are free to carry the charge (see Topic 7).

There are three acids that are used in standard grade. For each you must learn the names and formulas.

Acid	Formula	Ionic Formula
Hydrochloric Acid	HCl	$H^+_{(aq)} + Cl^-_{(aq)}$
Sulphuric Acid	H_2SO_4	$2H^+_{(aq)} + SO_4^{2-}_{(aq)}$
Nitric Acid	HNO_3	$H^+_{(aq)} + NO_3^-_{(aq)}$

When an acid is diluted with water the concentration of H^+ ions is decreased. This increases the pH of the solution toward 7 because the acid is becoming less acidic.

Remember acids are produced when non-metal oxides are dissolved in water.

Alkali Solutions

Alkaline solutions have a pH greater than 7. This is because they contain more OH^- ions than H^+ ions. OH^- ions are why alkalis react like they do and all alkaline solutions contain OH^- ions. Like acids, alkalis conduct electricity because they have ions that are free to carry the charge.

There are three main alkalis to learn for Standard Grade:

Alkali	Formula	Ionic Formula
Sodium Hydroxide	NaOH	$Na^+_{(aq)}$ + $OH^-_{(aq)}$
Magnesium Hydroxide	$Mg(OH)_2$	$Mg^{2+}_{(aq)}$ + $2OH^-_{(aq)}$
Ammonia	NH_3	$NH_4^+_{(aq)}$ + $OH^-_{(aq)}$

When an alkali is diluted with water the concentration of OH^- ions is decreased. This decreases the pH of the solution toward 7 because the alkali is becoming less alkaline.

Alkali solutions are produced when soluble metal oxides or hydroxides dissolve in water.

Any substance that neutralises an acid can be called a Base.

> ## TOP TIP!
> Learn the formulas of the common acids and alkali s shown in these tables. They regularly appear in the exam - especially the acids!

Neutral Solutions

Neutral solutions have equal concentrations of OH⁻ and H⁺ ions which cancel each other out. It is because of this small amount of ions that water can conduct electricity.

$$H^+ + OH^- \longrightarrow H_2O$$

Electrolysis of Acids

Acidic solutions contain hydrogen ions. When electricity is passed through an acidic solution these positively charged hydrogen ions are attracted to the negative electrode and hydrogen gas is produced. This is true of any acid.

The electrolysis of an acid produces hydrogen at the negative electrode.

The test for hydrogen is that it burns with a pop.

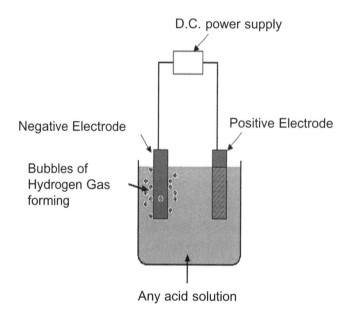

D.C. power supply

Negative Electrode

Positive Electrode

Bubbles of
Hydrogen Gas
forming

Any acid solution

The Mole

When you think of a mole you think of a small furry animal that lives under the ground. Not any more because in chemistry a mole is the gram formula mass of a substance.

The gram formula mass of a substance is known as one mole.

Listed on page 4 of your data booklet are the relative atomic mass numbers of selected elements. These can be used to calculate the gram formula mass of a substance.

For example, what is the mass of one mole of calcium chloride?

To calculate this all you have to do is work out the formula of calcium chloride. Then add all the mass numbers together. Remember to multiply if there is more than one atom, then put a g for gram after the number.

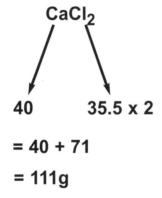

$CaCl_2$

40   35.5 x 2

= 40 + 71

= 111g

Example 2: What is the gram formula mass of sulphuric acid?

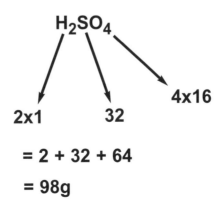

H_2SO_4

2x1   32   4x16

= 2 + 32 + 64

= 98g

Mole Calculations

Mole calculations can be easily done if this simple equation triangle is remembered.

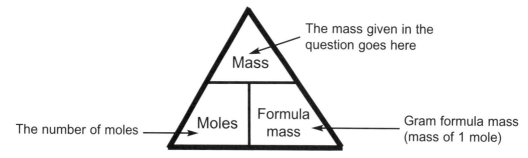

The mass given in the question goes here

The number of moles

Gram formula mass (mass of 1 mole)

For example:

How many moles are present in 25g of calcium carbonate?

Firstly the formula mass of calcium carbonate has to be calculated.

$$CaCO_3$$

40   12   3x16

= 40 + 12 + 48

= 100g

Mass = 25g
Moles = ?
Formula mass (FM)= 100g

$$Moles = \frac{mass}{FM} = \frac{25}{100} = \underline{\textbf{0.25 moles}}$$

More Calculations Involving Moles

Moles are also used to calculate concentrations of solutions. To do these calculations another equation triangle has to be learned.

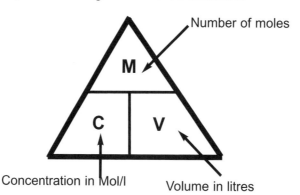

Number of moles

Concentration in Mol/l   Volume in litres

Calculate the concentration of a sulphuric acid solution if 2 moles are dissolved in 0.5l (500 cm³) of water.

C = ?
M = 2
V = 0.5l

Concentration $= \dfrac{M}{V} = \dfrac{2}{0.5} =$ **4 mol/l**

TOP TIP!
Everytime you see a concentration and a volume always multiply them together to find the number of moles.

The two calculations you have just learned can be combined to form one larger and slightly more difficult calculation.

Take your time to learn these as they are difficult!

What mass of sodium hydroxide is required to make 250 cm³ of 2mol/l sodium hydroxide solution?

First of all calculate the number of moles:

C = 2
M = ?
V = $\dfrac{250}{1000}$ = 0.25l

Number of moles = CxV = 2x0.25 = **0.5 moles**

(This can now be used to calculate the mass)

Now calculate the mass:

NaOH

23   16   1

= 23 + 16 + 1

= **40g**

Mass = ?
Moles = 0.5 moles
Formula mass (FM)= 40g

Mass = moles x FM = 40x0.5 = **20g**

TOPIC 9

NEUTRALISATION

Topic 8 dealt with acids and alkalis and the differences between them. Topic 9 tells us exactly what happens when we react these acids and alkalis together.

Neutralisation

Neutralisation is the reaction of an acid with a substance that moves its pH towards 7.

This moves the pH of the acid upwards ↑ towards 7 and the pH of the alkali downwards ↓ towards 7.

Neutralisation occurs everyday, for example, in the treatment of acid indigestion or adding lime to lakes to reduce their acidity.

Equations

There are 3 main equations for neutralisation all of which have to be learned.

Acid + Alkali ⟶ Salt + Water

Acid + Base ⟶ Salt + Water

Acid + Metal carbonate ⟶ Salt + Water + Carbon dioxide

A base is a substance that dissolves in water to produce an alkali - a soluble metal oxide (Topic 8).

Salt Names

A salt is the substance produced when an acid reacts with an alkali. Naming the salt is straightforward if you learn the table on the next page.

> **TOP TIP!**
> Remember this simple line to remember how to name salts.
> **Alkali to front, Acid to back!**

Acid	Salt Name Ends In...
HCl	...chloride
H_2SO_4	...sulphate
HNO_3	...nitrate

For Example:

Hydrochloric + **Sodium** ⟶ **Sodium** + **Water**
Acid **hydroxide** **chloride**

The salt is produced when the hydrogen ion of the acid is replaced by the metal ion of the alkali.

Why Is Water Produced?

During neutralisation the H^+ ion from the acid joins with the OH^- ion from the alkali. This is why water is formed in these reactions.

$$H^+ + OH^- \longrightarrow H_2O$$

This is true for most neutralisation reactions.

Other Acid Reactions

Acid and Metal Carbonate

When an acid reacts with any carbonate, carbon dioxide is produced.
For example:

$$2HCl + CaCO_3 \longrightarrow CaCl_2 + CO_2 + H_2O$$

The same method as before is used to name the salt.

REMEMBER!   Carbon Dioxide can be tested for using lime water
(turns from colourless to chalky white)

Acid and Metal

When an acid reacts with a reactive metal, salt and hydrogen gas is produced.
For example:

$$H_2SO_4 + Mg \longrightarrow MgSO_4 + H_2$$

The same method is used to name the salt.

REMEMBER!   To test for hydrogen, a lighted splint should burn with
a pop if hydrogen gas is present.

Ionic Equations

In Topic 8 you learned the ionic formulas of acids and alkalis. In Topic 9 they
have to be used to form ionic equations.

For Example:

$$HCl + NaOH \longrightarrow NaCl + H_2O$$

The ionic equation simply combines their ionic formulas.

For example:

$$H^+_{(aq)} + Cl^-_{(aq)} + Na^+_{(aq)} + OH^-_{(aq)} \longrightarrow Na^+_{(aq)} + Cl^-_{(aq)} + H_2O$$

This can be shortened further by removing the spectator ions. A spectator ion is like a spectator at the football. They are there at the game but are not taking part in the game. The spectator ions are ions that are present during the reaction but are unchanged by the reaction.

For example:

$$H^+_{(aq)} + \cancel{Cl^-_{(aq)}} + \cancel{Na^+_{(aq)}} + OH^-_{(aq)} \longrightarrow \cancel{Na^+_{(aq)}} + \cancel{Cl^-_{(aq)}} + H_2O$$

This leaves us with:

$$H^+_{(aq)} + OH^-_{(aq)} \longrightarrow H_2O$$

This is true for most neutralisation reactions.

Precipitation

Precipitation is the formation of an insoluble solid by reacting two liquids.

Put simply when two liquids are reacted together and a solid substance is produced it is called a precipitate.

> **TOP TIP!**
> A precipitate is always insoluble so use your data booklet to identify it.

Lead Nitrate + Sodium Iodide $\longrightarrow$ Sodium Nitrate + Lead Iodide

The precipitate is Lead iodide because it is an insoluble solid.

Titration Calculations

The concentrations of acids or alkalis can be calculated using titrations.

These are usually done in the lab from solutions known as Standard Solutions .
A Standard Solution is a solution with known concentration.

There are several ways to go about calculating the concentrations from
titrations but this is by far the easiest method. To make it easy to remember lets
call it the BIN BAG equation (PVC get it? - it certainly isn't a rubbish way to do it!)

$$PVC(acid) = PVC(alkali)$$

P = The number of H's the acid has or OH s the alkali has

V = The volume in litres

C = The concentration in mol/l

For Example:
What concentration is a Sulphuric acid solution if $500cm^3$ is neutralised by
$500 cm^3$ of 4 mol/l^{-1} sodium hydroxide?

$$PVC(acid) = PVC(alkali)$$

P = 2 (H_2SO_4)   **P** = 1 (NaOH)

V = $500cm^3$ = 0.5l   **V** = $500cm^3$ = 0.5l

C = ???????   **C** = 4 mol/l

$$2 \times 0.5 \times C = 1 \times 0.5 \times 4$$
$$1 \times C = 2$$
$$C = \frac{2}{1}$$
$$\underline{\underline{C = 2 \ mol/l}}$$

MAKING ELECTRICITY

Batteries are an essential part of our modern lives. They provide power for our mobile phones, our Mp3 players and even supply the energy to start our cars. Topic 10 explains how batteries work.

Batteries provide electricity for our use. To understand how a battery works we must know what electricity is.

Electricity is a flow of electrons that travel along wires.

In a battery this flow of electrons or electricity is produced by a chemical reaction taking place in the battery.

Batteries have one major disadvantage. They eventually run out. This happens when the chemicals in the battery are used up. Some batteries however are rechargeable like the lead-acid battery used in a car.

Reactivity Series

Before we can learn how a battery works it helps to know the reactivity series. The reactivity series is a list of metals listed in order of reactivity starting with the most reactive. It is very similar to the electrochemical series in your data booklet but with a few differences.

There is an easy way to remember the reactivity series if you learn the following story.

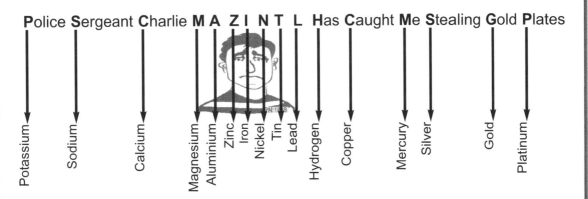

Police Sergeant Charlie M A Z I N T L Has Caught Me Stealing Gold Plates

Potassium, Sodium, Calcium, Magnesium, Aluminium, Zinc, Iron, Nickel, Tin, Lead, Hydrogen, Copper, Mercury, Silver, Gold, Platinum

Cell story (part 1)

This story is completely fictional but if you understand it topic 10 will become a lot easier.

> **Magnesium and Copper are cowboys in the old Wild West. To win the heart of a fair lady they challenge each other to an old fashioned 'shoot-out' at high noon. They meet at noon, stand back to back, walk twelve paces turn and shoot. BANG! Magnesium shoots copper dead with a bullet and wins the girl. Magnesium was the fastest to REACT!**

This story may seem out of place in a chemistry book but all will become clear as you read on.

The bullets mentioned in the story is a codeword for electrons. This means that the electrons are flowing from the magnesium (faster to react) to the copper (slower to react).

Most reactive
(faster to react)

Potassium
Sodium
Calcium
Magnesium
Aluminium
Zinc
Iron
Nickel
Tin
Lead
Hydrogen
Copper
Mercury
Silver
Gold

Least reactive
(slower to react)

Platinum

Electrons flow in this direction!

The electrons (bullets) will always go from the most reactive metal to the least reactive metal.

If electricity is a flow of electrons, then electricity is produced when this happens.

Cells

In chemistry a battery is known as a cell.

A cell is made up of two different metals connected by an electrolyte (to complete the circuit).

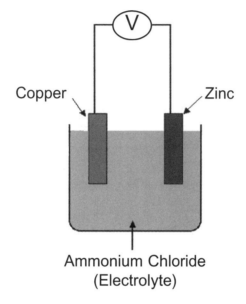

Copper

Zinc

Ammonium Chloride
(Electrolyte)

An electrolyte is an ionic solution that is used to complete the circuit.

The flow of electrons is produced because of the difference in reactivity of the two metals.

Electrons will flow from the most reactive metal to the least reactive metal.

So in the cell shown the electrons will flow from the zinc to the copper because zinc is more reactive than copper.

The further apart the metals are in the electrochemical series the higher the voltage produced.

So if we changed the zinc in the cell and replaced it with magnesium the voltage produced by the cell will increase because the magnesium is even more reactive than zinc.

Different Cells

There are several different ways in which cells can be made. Electricity can also be produced in a cell by connecting two different metals in solutions of their own ions.

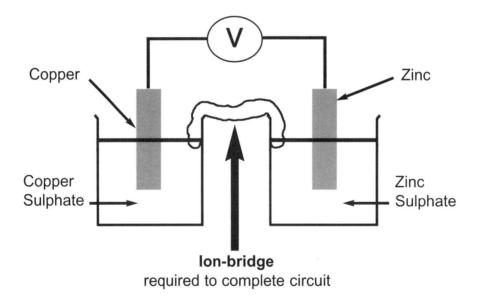

Ion-bridge
required to complete circuit

The electrons will flow from the zinc to the copper as in the previous cell. This will cause the zinc to form ions, and more copper to form on the surface of the copper electrode.

As with any electrical circuit it must be complete to work. The purpose of the ion bridge is to complete the circuit. The ion bridge is not some piece of high tech electrical equipment. It is simply a piece of filter paper soaked in salt water or some other ionic solution.

Another type of cell is one in which only one metal is involved and the other half of the cell contains SO_3^{2-} ions or I_2 with a carbon electrode. In most cells the electrons flow from the metal to the non-metal.

Cell story (part 2)

The story continues...

> After the 'shoot-out' Magnesium who was the winner, marries the fair lady and they both live happily ever after.
>
> **THE END**

What this story means is that the most reactive metal will ALWAYS get the girl . The girl is our code name for a group ion such as Sulphate or Nitrate. This story will help you understand the concept of displacement which we are about to cover.

Displacement Reactions

In displacement reactions a reactive metal displaces a metal that is less reactive from solution.

For example:

$$Mg + CuSO_4 \longrightarrow MgSO_4 + Cu \text{ (remember the story)}$$

The most reactive metal always 'gets the girl' (SO_4 in this case).

If the group ion is already combined to the most reactive metal then no reaction will occur.
For example:

$$Pb + ZnSO_4 \longrightarrow \text{No Reaction}$$

The most reactive metal is already joined to the group ion (girlfriend) and therefore no reaction will occur.

When a metal reacts with acid, hydrogen is released (displaced). This is also a displacement reaction and can be used to place hydrogen in the electrochemical series.

Oil Rig

As we have already found out substances can gain or lose electrons.

When substances lose electrons it is known as **oxidation**
When substances gain electrons it is known as **reduction**

There is an easy way to remember this using an Oil Rig.

O	Oxidation
I	Is
L	Loss
R	Reduction
I	Is
G	Gain

Oxidation
When an element is reacting to form a compound then it is being oxidised.

$$Mg \longrightarrow Mg^{2+} + 2e^-$$

The magnesium is losing 2 electrons so it is an oxidation reaction.

Reduction
Reduction is the opposite of oxidation. It is the gain of electrons.

$$Cu^{2+} + 2e^- \longrightarrow Cu$$

Redox

A redox reaction is one in which both oxidation and reduction take place.

All displacement reactions are redox reactions because one metal is gaining electrons (reduction) and one metal is losing electrons (oxidation).

METALS

Over three quarters of the elements known are metals. Topic 11 deals with their properties both physical and chemical.

From previous topics you should already be aware that all metals in the periodic table are on the left hand side of the 'zigzag line'. You should also know that all metals conduct electricity.

Density

Density is the mass of a substance in a given volume.

To explain better what this statement actually means try to answer this question.

Q: What is heavier lead or feathers?

If you answered lead then you may be wrong because you don't know how much feathers or lead you actually had.

I will ask the question again.

Q: What is heavier 1 litre of lead or 1 litre of feathers?

If you answered lead this time then you are correct, because in this question you are given a volume of both substances (1 Litre). This is called density!

Malleability

Malleability is the ability of a substance to be shaped or rolled into sheets.

This means that if a substance can be shaped by a hammer for example, or rolled into sheets, then it is said to be malleable. Most metals are malleable.

Reactions Of Metals

Metals and Water

Most metals do not react with water but some of the more reactive metals do.

For example:
The alkali metals lithium, sodium and potassium react very strongly and caesium can even explode in water. (Topic 3)

Reactive   +   Water   ———————➤   Metal   +   Hydrogen
Metal   Hydroxide

However some metals can react very slowly with water when air is present like copper and iron.

Gold, silver and platinum do not react with water at all.

Reactions with Acids

As before, it is the more reactive metals that will react with acids. Think back to Topic 10, only the metals above hydrogen in the reactivity series react with acid, because all acids contain H^+ ions. Acids will not have an effect on metals such as gold and platinum.

Metal + Acid   ———————➤   Salt + Hydrogen (Topic 9)

Reactions with Oxygen

Again only the most reactive metals react strongly with oxygen and the least reactive metals are unchanged (there is no reaction).

For Example:
In class you may have burned magnesium. This reacts very strongly with oxygen to give off a bright light (exothermic reaction).

Metal + Oxygen   ———————➤   Metal oxide

Extraction of Metals

Metals are a finite resource. When a source of a metal has been discovered it is not found as a pure metal, but as part of a compound. This means that over a period of time the metal will have reacted with oxygen in the air and water.

When metals are found in this state they are called ores.

The less reactive metals such as gold and platinum are found as a pure metal because they are very unreactive. All other metals have to be removed from their ores.

Unreactive metals are easy to remove from their ores. However, the more reactive the metal the more difficult it is to remove.

Shown is a table of what process must be undertaken to remove metals from their ores. This a common question in the exam so learn the table.

METAL	PROCESS
Potassium Sodium Lithium Calcium Magnesium Aluminium	Electrolysis
Zinc	
Iron	Blast Furnace
Nickel Tin Lead Copper	Heating with Carbon or CO
Mercury Silver Gold Platinum	Heat alone

The unreactive metals are removed from their ores simply by heating. Metals such as Zinc, Nickel, Tin, Lead and Copper need to be heated with carbon (or CO) to remove them. The more reactive metals require electrolysis to achieve this (Topic 7). Iron however is removed in a blast furnace.

The Blast Furnace

Iron is extracted from it's ore in the blast furnace. The blast furnace is a complex process that involves two main stages.

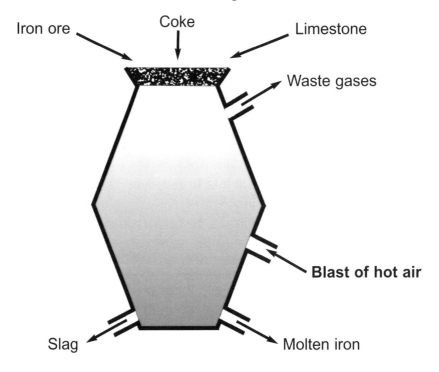

Stage 1
Iron ore, Coke (which is a form of carbon) and limestone are fed into the top of the blast furnace. The limestone is required to remove any impurities.

Stage 2
A blast (see where the name blast furnace comes from?) of hot air is fed into the bottom of the furnace. This is required to provide oxygen so that the carbon (coke) undergoes incomplete combustion to give carbon monoxide:

$$C \ + \ O_2 \longrightarrow CO_2$$
$$CO_2 \ + \ C \longrightarrow 2CO$$

The carbon monoxide produced is then used to remove the oxygen from the iron(III)oxide (iron ore) to produce iron.

$$Fe_2O_3 \ + 3CO \longrightarrow 2Fe \ + \ 3CO_2$$

The temperatures inside the blast furnace are so high that the iron produced is molten and falls to the bottom of the furnace where it is run off.

Alloys

When you hear the word alloy you may think of a fancy type of wheel on a car but there is a lot more to alloys than that.

An alloy is a selection of metals, mixed together to give them the properties required to do a specific job. This means that there are a lot of different forms of alloys, all of which have specific properties for a specific purpose.

For example:
Stainless steel and brass are two examples of alloys but with very different properties.

Empirical Formula

The empirical formula of a compound is the simplest formula obtained from experimental data. It is very simple if you follow this method:

4.78g of lead oxide was reduced to give 4.14g of lead metal, use this information to work out the empirical formula for the lead oxide.

Symbol	Pb	O
Weight	4.14	0.64
Divide by formula mass	$\dfrac{4.14}{207}$ =0.02	$\dfrac{0.64}{16}$ =0.04
Divide by smallest number	$\dfrac{0.02}{0.02}$ =1	$\dfrac{0.04}{0.02}$ =2
Formula	PbO_2	

TOPIC 12

CORROSION

Corrosion is the reaction of a metal with oxygen and water. Corrosion of iron is more commonly known as rust. Topic 12 deals with the causes of corrosion and how it can be prevented.

What Causes Corrosion?

Different metals corrode at different rates depending on the reactivity of the metal.

The common name for corrosion is rusting. This is wrong because only iron rusts, all other metals corrode. Although they are the same reaction, when iron corrodes it is referred to as rusting.

There are two substances required for a metal to corrode, oxygen and water.

Some substances increase the rate of corrosion such as salt and acid rain. This is because the electrolytes and the ions quickly carry the electrons away.

What Happens When Metals Corrode?

When iron corrodes the iron atoms lose electrons to form ions. **This is called oxidation.** (Topic 10).

$$Fe \longrightarrow Fe^{2+} + 2e^-$$

When you hear the word rust you picture the red/orange substance on the bodies of old cars. The substance you are thinking of is iron oxide. When iron rusts this is the substance it forms.

The Fe^{2+} ions produced in the previous reaction can lose another electron to form Fe^{3+} ions. This means that Fe^{2+} ions can be further oxidised.

$$Fe^{2+} \longrightarrow Fe^{3+} + e$$

64

Redox

As we learned in Topic 10, there can't be oxidation without reduction.

The electrons lost by the iron during rusting must be gained by another substance, or substances.

The electrons lost by the iron during rusting are gained by the oxygen and water molecules to form hydroxide ions.
For Example:

$$2H_2O_{(l)} + O_{2(g)} + 4e^- \longrightarrow 4OH^-_{(aq)}$$

> **TOP TIP!**
> This equation is in the data booklet you will be given in the exam.

Ferroxyl Indicator

The indicator used to test for corrosion is Ferroxyl Indicator.

Ferroxyl indicator turns blue in the presence of Fe^{2+} ions and turns pink when OH^- ions are present.

For Example:

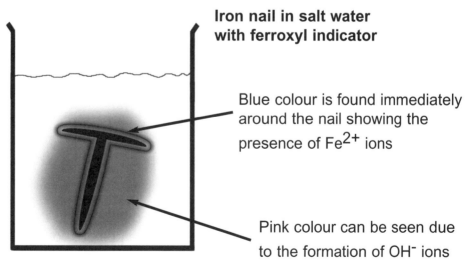

Iron nail in salt water with ferroxyl indicator

Blue colour is found immediately around the nail showing the presence of Fe^{2+} ions

Pink colour can be seen due to the formation of OH^- ions

Both colours will be displayed because when rusting occurs both iron ions and hydroxide ions are formed. This results in a blue colour being formed around the iron nail and a pink colour being formed in the water.

Protection from Corrosion

Protection from corrosion is a very big business. There are several different ways to protect metals from corrosion some of which are listed below.

Physical Protection

A simple way of protecting a metal from corrosion is by preventing the oxygen and water from reaching the metals surface. This can be done in several ways such as painting the metal, coating it in grease or oil, or coating it with a plastic material. All of these methods act as a shield, protecting the metal from oxygen and water.

Cathodic Protection

When iron rusts it loses electrons. A method of protection is to attach the metal to the negative terminal of a battery. This will give a constant supply of electrons to the metal preventing it from losing them.

> ### TOP TIP!
> Remember that the metal must be attached to the negative electrode. As the positive electrode would take electrons from the metal speeding up the rate of corrosion.

Galvanising

Galvanising is the coating of zinc onto iron or steel. This provides a physical barrier, however if this is broken then the zinc will provide sacrificial protection for the iron or steel (see next page).

Electroplating

Electroplating is the coating of gold, silver, copper or some other unreactive metal onto metal objects.

This is done by connecting the object that is to be plated, to the negative electrode of a D.C. power supply and dipping the object into a solution of gold, silver or copper ions (Topic 7 Electrolysis). The positive metal ions are attracted to the object and form a layer of the solid metal on the object that is being coated.

Sacrificial protection

In Topic 10 we discovered that metals lose electrons to metals less reactive than themselves when connected in a cell. This can be used to protect a metal from corrosion.

For example:
When Iron is corroding it loses electrons. If it is attached to a more reactive metal, then it will be supplied with electrons preventing the iron from corrosion. This is known as sacrificial protection because a metal is being sacrificed to protect another.

This can be shown using ferroxyl indicator. In an iron/zinc cell the zinc loses electrons to the iron. This is shown by the **pink colour** formed around the iron electrode. If the iron was losing electrons then a **blue colour** would be formed around the iron electrode, because the ferroxyl indicator only turns blue in the presence of Fe^{2+} ions

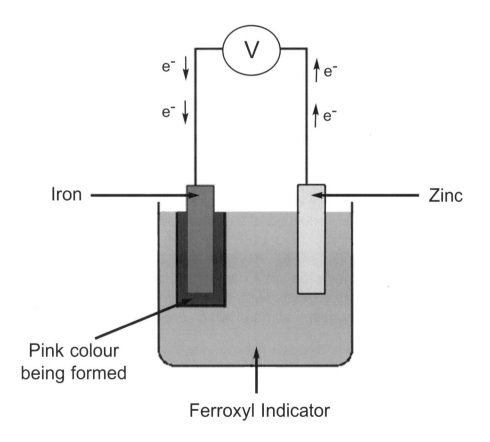

TOPIC 13

PLASTICS

There are many different types of plastics all with very different properties. These properties give them a massive range of uses from clothing to packaging to children's toys. Topic 13 highlights the advantages and disadvantages of plastics as well as looking at how plastics are produced.

Natural or Synthetic

Synthetic is the name given to all materials that are man made. All plastics are synthetic compounds made mainly from the crude oil fraction, naptha.

They are made by a process called polymerisation which we will deal with later in the topic.

There are many advantages of plastics over natural materials and some disadvantages. For example cotton (natural) is far more comfortable to wear, but nylon (synthetic) is far more hardwearing.

Pollution

Plastics have many advantages over natural products but they have one major disadvantage and that is pollution.

Plastics are not biodegradable. This means that they do not rot away naturally. This can cause long term litter problems because the plastics disposed of in this way will be around for a very very long time. Recent developments of plastics have resulted in the production of biodegradable plastics such as Biopol.

When plastics are burned they produce a dangerous form of pollution. When they burn they all produce toxic gases such as carbon monoxide. Some plastics can also produce other toxic gases some of which are listed on the next page.

Plastics	Toxic Gas Produced
Polystyrene or any plastic	Carbon monoxide
PVC	Hydrogen chloride (HCl) + Carbon monoxide
Polyurethane (used as a foam in chairs)	Hydrogen cyanide (HCN) + Carbon monoxide

Thermoplastics and Thermosetting plastics

There are two main categories of plastic.

Thermoplastic - **A plastic that will soften on heating and can be reshaped.**

Thermosetting - **A plastic that will not soften on heating.**

Addition Polymerisation

Polymerisation is a process by which many small molecules called monomers combine to form one large molecule called a polymer (the plastic).

Monomer - The small molecules that combine to form the polymer.

Polymer - **The large molecule formed by combining many monomer molecules.**

Addition polymerisation is just one way in which plastics are produced.
In Topic 6 we learned about addition reactions with alkenes and bromine. The concept is the same for addition polymerisation but on a much larger scale.

For example:
The ethene monomers add across the double bonds.

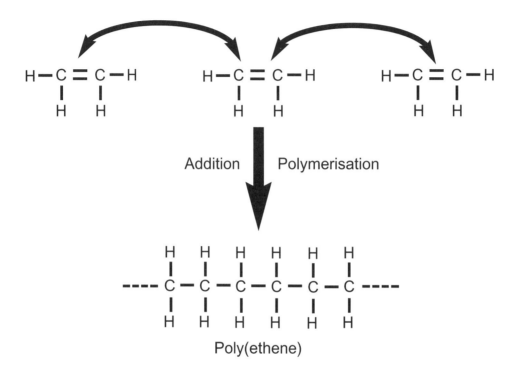

Poly(ethene)

The ethene monomers add to each other across the double bond to form the polymer polyethene.

Addition polymerisation is the addition of monomer molecules across their double bonds, therefore for this process to work **the monomers for addition polymerisation must be unsaturated** (double bond Topic 6).

To name the polymer produced is very simple, just add **poly** to the start of the monomer name.
For example:

> **Ethene produces poly(ethene)**
>
> **Propene produces poly(propene)**
>
> **Butene produces poly(butene)**

Because the polymer molecules produced are very large, chemists have developed what is known as the repeating unit. This is a shorted version of the polymer molecule.

For example:
The poly(ethene) molecule shown is very large. The repeating unit makes things a bit simpler.

$$\left(\begin{array}{ccc} & H & H \\ & | & | \\ - & C - C - \\ & | & | \\ & H & H \end{array} \right)_n$$

Where 'n' is any large number

Poly(propene) has the repeating unit

$$\left(\begin{array}{ccc} & H & CH_3 \\ & | & | \\ - & C - C - \\ & | & | \\ & H & H \end{array} \right)_n$$

TOPIC 14

FERTILISERS

Fertilisers are required for the production of crops. Topic 14 highlights what a fertiliser is and how they are produced.

Year on year the world population is increasing which has led to a larger demand on food production. This has resulted in the need for fertilisers which are capable of producing the food required to meet these high demands.

What Is A Fertiliser?

Fertilisers provide the three main nutrients that plants require to grow well. The three main nutrients are:

Nitrogen (N)
Phosphorus (P)
Potassium (K)

There are two main types of fertiliser:

Natural fertilisers   Natural fertilisers provide mainly nitrogen compounds and include things such as manure and compost.

Synthetic fertilisers   Synthetic (man made) fertilisers provide all three nutrients in varying amounts, but can be expensive.

Leguminous Plants

Leguminous plants are a special type of plant that can convert nitrogen from the air (remember the air is about 79% nitrogen) into nitrogen compounds that they can then use to provide themselves with nutrients.

These plants have root nodules that contain nitrifying bacteria. These nitrifying bacteria are capable of converting nitrogen from the air into soluble nitrogen compounds that the plant can use as nutrients.

Peas, beans and clover are all leguminous plants and farmers use them to replace nitrogen in their soil rather than using expensive fertilisers.

Clover

Root nodules that contain nitrifying bacteria can convert atmospheric nitrogen into soluble nitrogen compounds, that the plant uses to provide the essential nutrient - **Nitrogen.**

Pollution

Fertilisers are not perfect. They can cause pollution problems. This is because for plants to absorb these nutrients through their root systems the nutrients must be soluble. If these nutrients are washed away into river systems by heavy rain then the plants in the rivers will absorb these nutrients causing accelerated growth. This leads to low oxygen levels in the water which can damage the wildlife in these systems.

Nitrogen Cycle

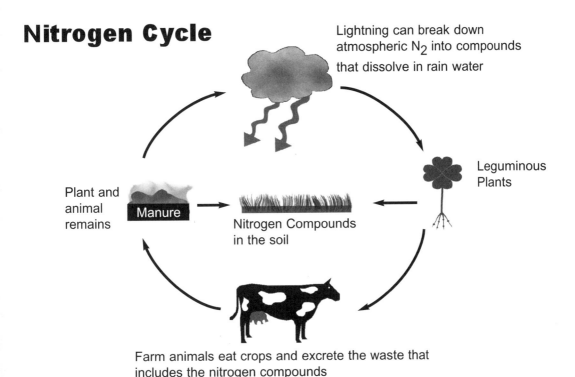

Lightning can break down atmospheric N_2 into compounds that dissolve in rain water

Leguminous Plants

Plant and animal remains

Manure

Nitrogen Compounds in the soil

Farm animals eat crops and excrete the waste that includes the nitrogen compounds

Ammonia

Ammonia is a very important chemical in the fertiliser industry. It is used **as a fertiliser** and can also be used to make other fertilisers. As we discovered in Topic 8, ammonia solution is alkaline with a very unpleasant smell. It is produced in industry by the 'Haber Process'.

The Haber Process

The Haber process produces ammonia (NH_3) by combining nitrogen and hydrogen. The nitrogen required comes from the air, and the hydrogen from methane. They are converted into ammonia by passing them over an **iron catalyst** at a moderately high temperature of $500^{\circ}C$ using high pressure. These conditions are chosen because at low temperatures the reaction is very slow. However, at high temperatures the ammonia breaks back down into hydrogen and nitrogen too quickly because the reaction is reversible.

$$N_{2(g)} + 3H_{2(g)} \rightleftharpoons 2NH_{3(g)}$$

Because not all the nitrogen and hydrogen are converted into ammonia they are put back recycled into the reaction chamber to make the whole process more economic. Nothing is wasted.

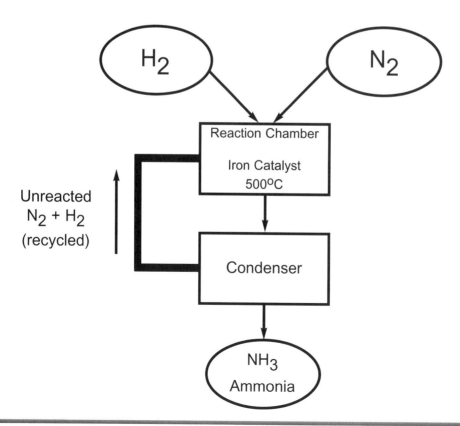

Ammonia can also be produced in the lab by heating any ammonium compound with an alkali. Ammonium salts are produced by reacting ammonia with an acid.

The Ostwald Process (oxidation of ammonia)

In Topic 5 we learned that oxides of nitrogen contribute to acid rain. This is because when nitrogen dioxide dissolves in water it forms nitric acid. Nitric acid can have useful properties however, as it can also be used in the production of fertilisers.

Producing nitric acid in the lab is a difficult process because nitrogen is very unreactive due to its strong triple bond. However it can be done by sparking air like the spark plugs in a car engine (it also happens naturally in lightning storms) but this is very expensive. The more economic way is by the **Ostwald Process.**

This involves passing ammonia (from the Haber process) and air over a **platinum catalyst** at a high temperature of 800°C. This produces nitrogen monoxide which combines with oxygen to form nitrogen dioxide. This can easily be converted into nitric acid by dissolving in water.

The Ostwald process is an **exothermic reaction** so once the reaction has started the heat can be removed and the catalyst will continue to glow red hot.

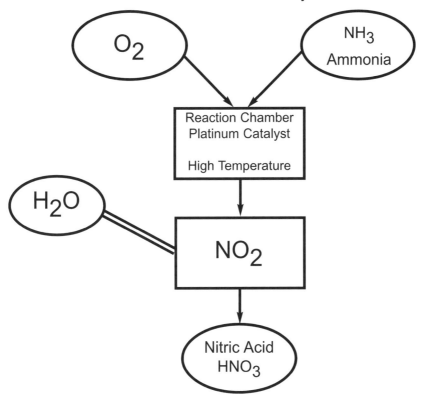

Percentage Composition Calculations

Chemists often need to know the amount of an element in compounds, which is particularly important when talking about fertilisers.

This is known as percentage composition.

For example:
Q: Ammonium nitrate is a commonly used fertiliser, what percentage of ammonium nitrate is nitrogen?

These calculations are straightforward if you follow this method.

Step 1 - Work out the formula and the formula mass of ammonium nitrate
Step 2 - Calculate the mass of nitrogen in the compound
Step 3 - Use this information to calculate the percentage composition

Ammonium nitrate

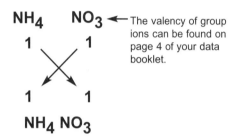

Formula mass calculation

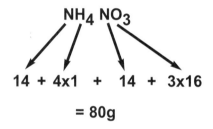

$$14 + 4\times1 \; + \; 14 + 3\times16$$
$$= 80g$$

Percentage composition

$$\% \text{ nitrogen} = \frac{\text{mass of nitrogen}}{\text{Formula mass}} = \frac{28}{80} = 35\%$$

A: The percentage nitrogen in ammonium nitrate is 35%.

Note: total mass of nitrogen in the compound is 28g because there are 2 nitrogen atoms in the formula (2 x 14 = 28).

CARBOHYDRATES

Carbohydrates are an essential part of our diet, but the way in which they are produced is essential in maintaining the balance of gases in our atmosphere.

Plants make carbohydrates which are high energy foods containing the elements carbon, hydrogen and oxygen. They do this by the method of **photosynthesis.**

Photosynthesis

During photosynthesis plants absorb carbon dioxide from the atmosphere and water through their root systems. Oxygen is produced for us to breathe, and carbohydrates are produced which we can use to provide us with energy.

The balanced equation for this reaction is:

$$6CO_2 + 6H_2O \longrightarrow C_6H_{12}O_6 + 6O_2$$
$$\text{(Glucose)}$$

Photosynthesis takes place in the leaves of plants. The green substance called Chlorophyll absorbs light energy which is essential for photosynthesis to occur.

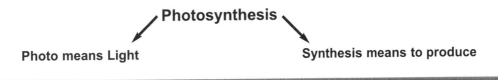

Photosynthesis

Photo means Light   **Synthesis means to produce**

Respiration

Animals (that includes humans too) obtain energy by breaking down carbohydrates. This is achieved by the carbohydrate reacting with oxygen. This produces the energy we require to live, however it also produces the waste products, carbon dioxide and water. Respiration is the opposite of photosynthesis.

The equation for respiration is:

$$C_6H_{12}O_6 + 6O_2 \longrightarrow 6CO_2 + 6H_2O$$
(Glucose)

Pollution

Photosynthesis and respiration are important in maintaining a balance of carbon dioxide and water in the atmosphere. What animals breathe out, plants take in.

However, burning fossil fuels has increased the level of carbon dioxide in our atmosphere and clearing forests has resulted in less plants to remove this extra carbon dioxide. This has resulted in global warming which is more commonly known as the greenhouse effect.

Sugars

Sugars are an important part of our diet because they provide a high degree of energy. All sugars contain the elements, carbon, hydrogen and oxygen which is why they are classed as carbohydrates.

There are three groups of sugar:

Type	Names	Formula
Monosaccharides	Glucose Fructose	$C_6H_{12}O_6$
Disaccharides	Maltose Sucrose	$C_{12}H_{22}O_{11}$
Polysaccharides	Starch Cellulose	$(C_{12}H_{10}O_5)n$

TOP TIP!
Learn the names and formulas of each sugar.

You may be asking the question, how can two sugars such as glucose and fructose have the same formula? This is because they are ISOMERS (Topic 6). They have the same molecular formula but different structural formula.

Tests

There are some simple tests that can be performed to identify the sugars. Benedict's solution is an indicator that turns from blue to orange in the presence of Glucose, Fructose or Maltose. These are called reducing sugars. However starch and sucrose have no effect on benedict's solution. There is however a test for starch. It reacts with iodine solution turning it from brown to black.

	Fructose	Glucose	Maltose	Sucrose	Starch
Benedict s Solution	Turns from **blue** to **orange**	Turns from **blue** to **orange**	Turns from **blue** to **orange**	No reaction	No reaction
Iodine Solution	No reaction	No reaction	No reaction	No reaction	Turns from **brown** to **black**

Condensation Polymerisation

TOP TIP!
Read over addition polymerisation in Topic 13 before you read on.

The polysaccharides are formed by condensation polymerisation. This is similar to addition polymerisation but this time water is formed as well as the polymer molecule. The polysaccharides are formed when many glucose molecules combine. This is performed in plants after photosynthesis to produce starch.

The glucose molecules:

Stage 1
The glucose molecules lose water

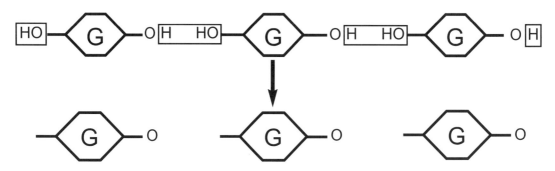

Stage 2
The glucose molecules combine
to form starch

Remember the diagram shown above is on a very small scale. These polymers are very large in real life.

Both starch and cellulose are insoluble in water this is due to their very large molecular size. They are simply too big to fit in between the water molecules. This can be shown by the Tyndall Effect. When a beam of light is passed through a glucose solution the beam passes directly through, however when this is repeated with a starch solution, the solution appears to become cloudy. This is because the starch molecules are so large that they reflect the light. **For example:**

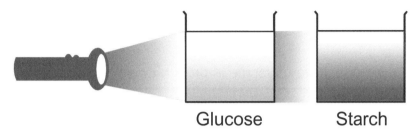

Glucose   Starch

Digestion

Digestion is the process by which the body gets the energy it needs from the food that we eat. During digestion large molecules are broken down into smaller molecules that can pass through the gut wall.

> ### TOP TIP!
> Imagine the gut wall to be like a sieve and the starch molecules are strings of spaghetti.

These large starch molecules are broken down by biological catalysts called enzymes. For example:

Stage 1
The starch molecules enter the body

Stage 2 (amylase)
The enzymes act like hammers to break down the starch into glucose

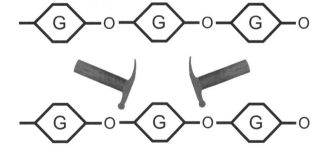

Stage 3
The glucose molecules are small enough to pass through the gut wall into the blood stream

Blood stream

Enzymes are biological catalysts and because of this they work best at body temperature ($37^\circ C$).

The process of breaking down starch can be done in the lab using concentrated acid at $100^\circ C$ but is a faster reaction when using enzymes at body temperature.

In chemistry the process of breaking down starch into glucose is known as hydrolysis.

Hydrolysis is when one large molecule is broken down into smaller molecules by reaction with water.

Hydrolysis is the reverse reaction of condensation polymerisation because water is added to a large molecule to break it into smaller molecules.

Alcohol

Alcohol is produced by sugar reacting to produce ethanol and carbon dioxide. This is known as **fermentation**.

For the reaction to take place an enzyme must be used. The enzymes used for alcohol production are contained in yeast. The enzyme is called Zymase. The equation for the final stage of the reaction is as follows:

$$C_6H_{12}O_6 \longrightarrow 2CO_2 + 2C_2H_5OH$$

Because an enzyme is used the reaction must be carried out at body temperature. Fermentation only produces alcohol to a maximum concentration of about 12%. This is because at this concentration the enzyme in the yeast dies and therefore the reaction is finished.

Drinks with high alcohol content such as whisky and vodka however, are produced by the process of **distillation**. This process involves collecting the 12% concentration solution produced by fermentation and heating it to about $78^\circ C$. At this temperature the alcohol boils and evaporates leaving behind the water. The alcohol is then cooled and collected. This increases the alcohol concentration greatly.

Mind Maps

The following Mind Maps are designed to aid your revision by providing a fun and easy way of remembering the most important study points from each topic of Standard Grade Chemistry.

Mind Maps show you the structure of the topic as well as the raw facts contained within this study guide. Mind Maps hold information in a format that your mind will find easy to remember and quick to review.

Mind Maps help you to make associations easily, but it is important to remember that they are simply a study aid and learning them alone does not offer sufficient detail to be successful in your exam.

TOPIC 1
Chemical Reactions

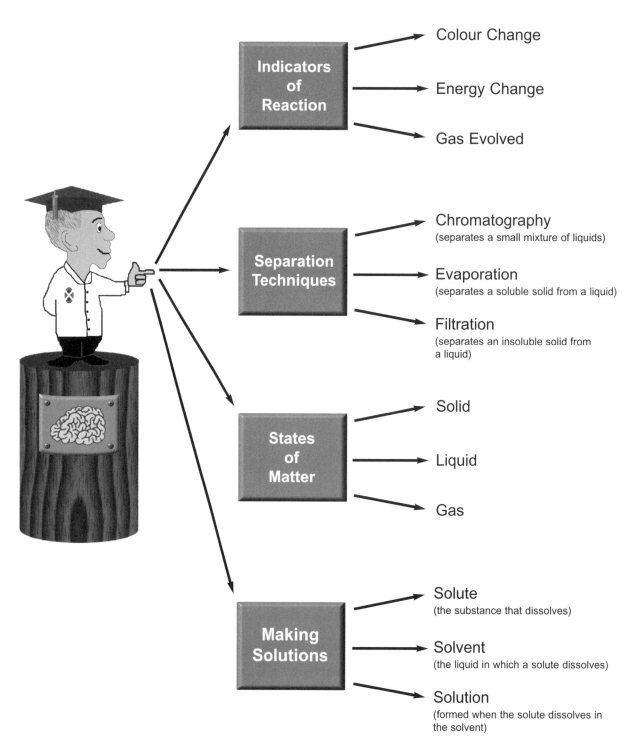

Indicators of Reaction
- Colour Change
- Energy Change
- Gas Evolved

Separation Techniques
- Chromatography (separates a small mixture of liquids)
- Evaporation (separates a soluble solid from a liquid)
- Filtration (separates an insoluble solid from a liquid)

States of Matter
- Solid
- Liquid
- Gas

Making Solutions
- Solute (the substance that dissolves)
- Solvent (the liquid in which a solute dissolves)
- Solution (formed when the solute dissolves in the solvent)

TOPIC 2
Rate of Reactions

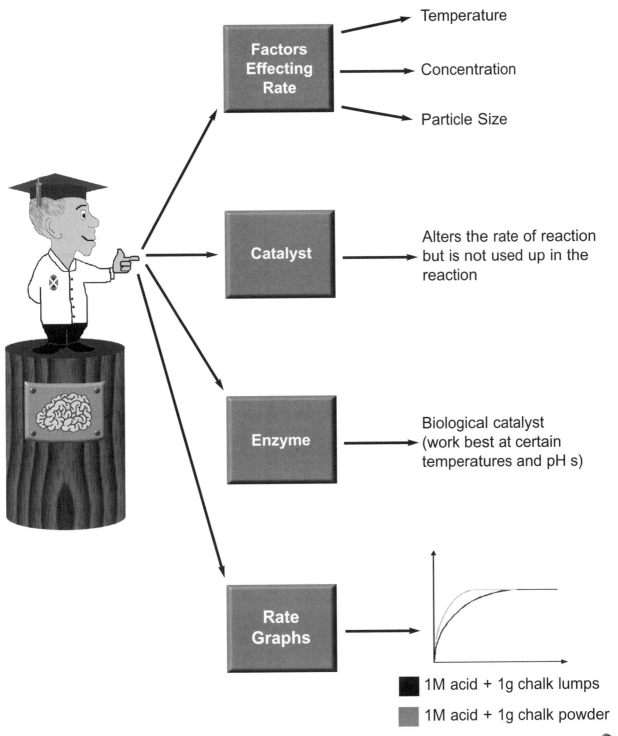

Factors Effecting Rate
- Temperature
- Concentration
- Particle Size

Catalyst → Alters the rate of reaction but is not used up in the reaction

Enzyme → Biological catalyst (work best at certain temperatures and pH s)

Rate Graphs →

■ 1M acid + 1g chalk lumps

■ 1M acid + 1g chalk powder

TOPIC 3
Atoms & The Periodic Table

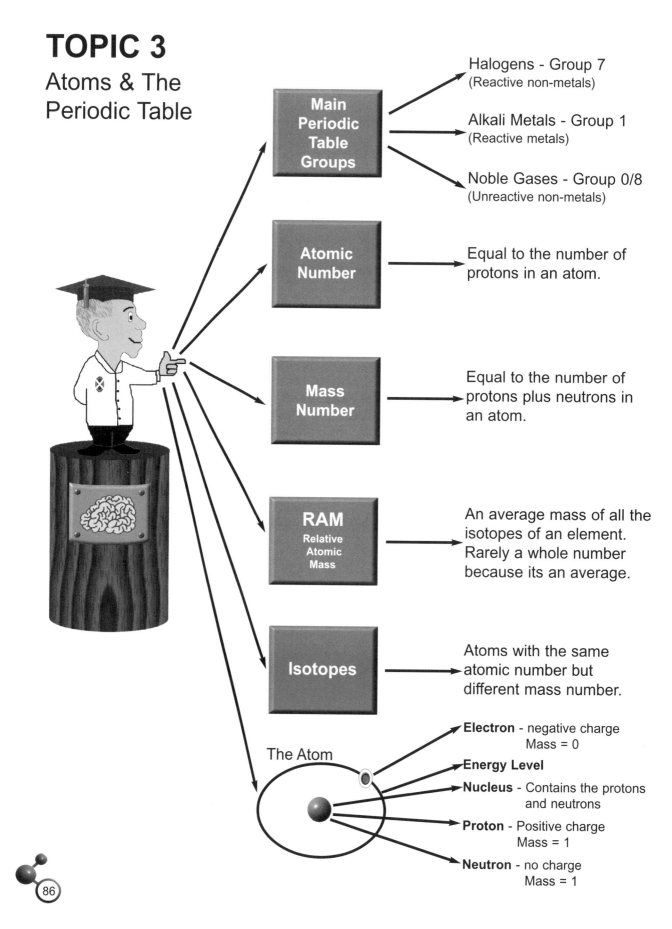

Main Periodic Table Groups

Halogens - Group 7
(Reactive non-metals)

Alkali Metals - Group 1
(Reactive metals)

Noble Gases - Group 0/8
(Unreactive non-metals)

Atomic Number

Equal to the number of protons in an atom.

Mass Number

Equal to the number of protons plus neutrons in an atom.

RAM
Relative Atomic Mass

An average mass of all the isotopes of an element. Rarely a whole number because its an average.

Isotopes

Atoms with the same atomic number but different mass number.

The Atom

Electron - negative charge
Mass = 0

Energy Level

Nucleus - Contains the protons and neutrons

Proton - Positive charge
Mass = 1

Neutron - no charge
Mass = 1

TOPIC 4
How Atoms Combine

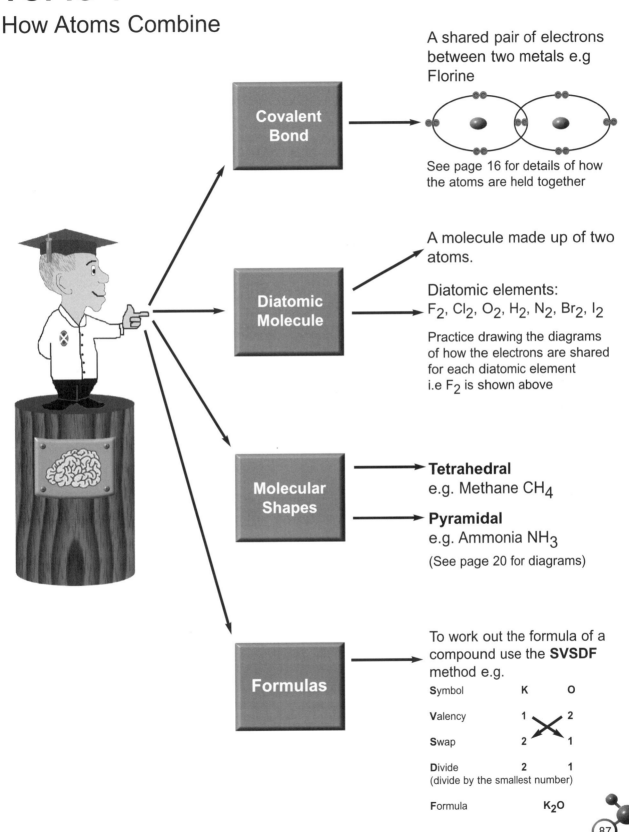

Covalent Bond

A shared pair of electrons between two metals e.g Florine

See page 16 for details of how the atoms are held together

Diatomic Molecule

A molecule made up of two atoms.

Diatomic elements:
F_2, Cl_2, O_2, H_2, N_2, Br_2, I_2

Practice drawing the diagrams of how the electrons are shared for each diatomic element i.e F_2 is shown above

Molecular Shapes

Tetrahedral
e.g. Methane CH_4

Pyramidal
e.g. Ammonia NH_3
(See page 20 for diagrams)

Formulas

To work out the formula of a compound use the **SVSDF** method e.g.

Symbol	K	O
Valency	1	2
Swap	2	1
Divide	2	1
(divide by the smallest number)		
Formula		K_2O

TOPIC 5
Fuels

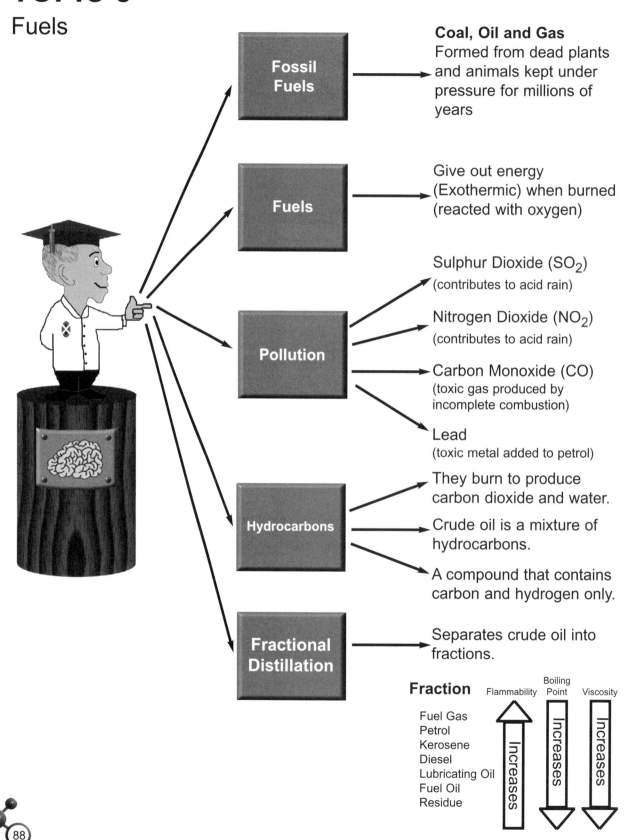

Fossil Fuels

Coal, Oil and Gas
Formed from dead plants and animals kept under pressure for millions of years

Fuels

Give out energy (Exothermic) when burned (reacted with oxygen)

Pollution

Sulphur Dioxide (SO_2)
(contributes to acid rain)

Nitrogen Dioxide (NO_2)
(contributes to acid rain)

Carbon Monoxide (CO)
(toxic gas produced by incomplete combustion)

Lead
(toxic metal added to petrol)

Hydrocarbons

They burn to produce carbon dioxide and water.

Crude oil is a mixture of hydrocarbons.

A compound that contains carbon and hydrogen only.

Fractional Distillation

Separates crude oil into fractions.

Fraction

Fuel Gas
Petrol
Kerosene
Diesel
Lubricating Oil
Fuel Oil
Residue

Flammability — Increases

Boiling Point — Increases

Viscosity — Increases

TOPIC 6
Hydrocarbons

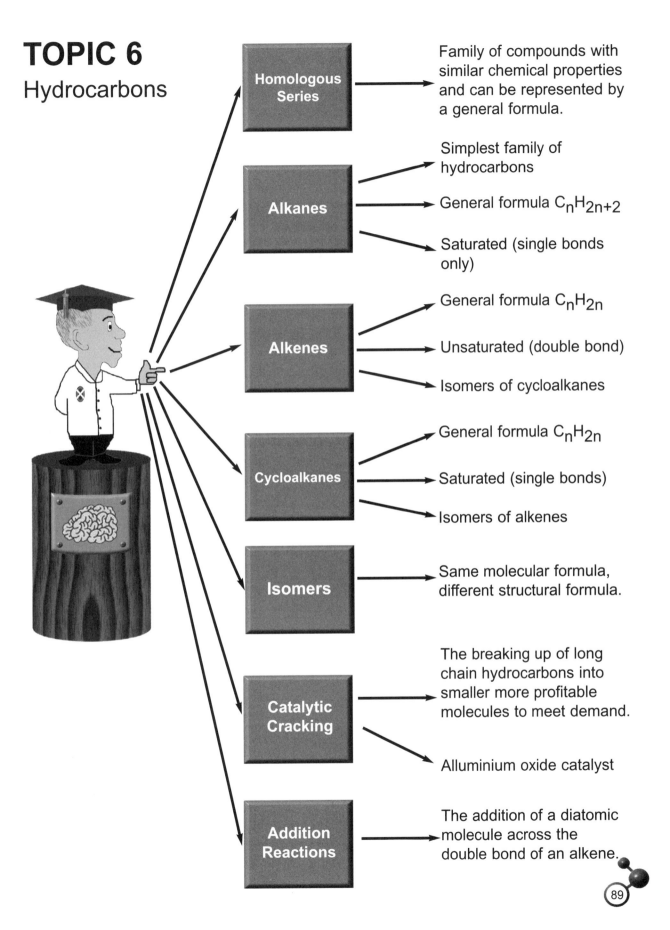

Homologous Series → Family of compounds with similar chemical properties and can be represented by a general formula.

Alkanes →
- Simplest family of hydrocarbons
- General formula C_nH_{2n+2}
- Saturated (single bonds only)

Alkenes →
- General formula C_nH_{2n}
- Unsaturated (double bond)
- Isomers of cycloalkanes

Cycloalkanes →
- General formula C_nH_{2n}
- Saturated (single bonds)
- Isomers of alkenes

Isomers → Same molecular formula, different structural formula.

Catalytic Cracking →
- The breaking up of long chain hydrocarbons into smaller more profitable molecules to meet demand.
- Alluminium oxide catalyst

Addition Reactions → The addition of a diatomic molecule across the double bond of an alkene.

TOPIC 7

Properties of Substances

Ions

→ A charged particle.

→ Metals form positive charges.

→ Non metals form negative charges.

Electrolysis

→ The breaking up of an ionic compound using electricity.

Ion Migration

→ Ions can be seen to move to their oppositely charged electrode (See page 38).

Ionic Formula

→ The formula of a compound showing the charges on each ion in the compound e.g.

$$Na^+_{(aq)} \quad + \quad OH^-_{(aq)}$$

Properties

→

	Ionic Lattice	Covalent Network	Discrete Covalent Molecule
Boiling Point	High	Very High	Low
State at Room Temperature	Solid	Solid	Liquid or Gas
Conduction of Electricity	ONLY when molten or in solution	Never (except graphite)	Never

TOPIC 8
Acids & Alkalis

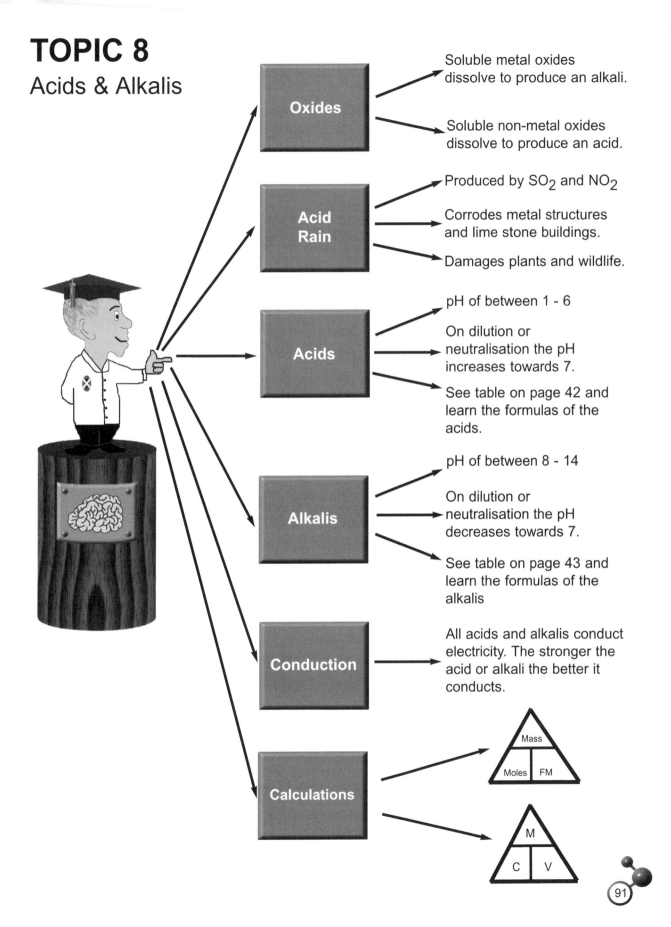

Oxides
- Soluble metal oxides dissolve to produce an alkali.
- Soluble non-metal oxides dissolve to produce an acid.

Acid Rain
- Produced by SO_2 and NO_2
- Corrodes metal structures and lime stone buildings.
- Damages plants and wildlife.

Acids
- pH of between 1 - 6
- On dilution or neutralisation the pH increases towards 7.
- See table on page 42 and learn the formulas of the acids.

Alkalis
- pH of between 8 - 14
- On dilution or neutralisation the pH decreases towards 7.
- See table on page 43 and learn the formulas of the alkalis

Conduction
All acids and alkalis conduct electricity. The stronger the acid or alkali the better it conducts.

Calculations

Mass / Moles / FM

M / C / V

TOPIC 9
Neutralisation

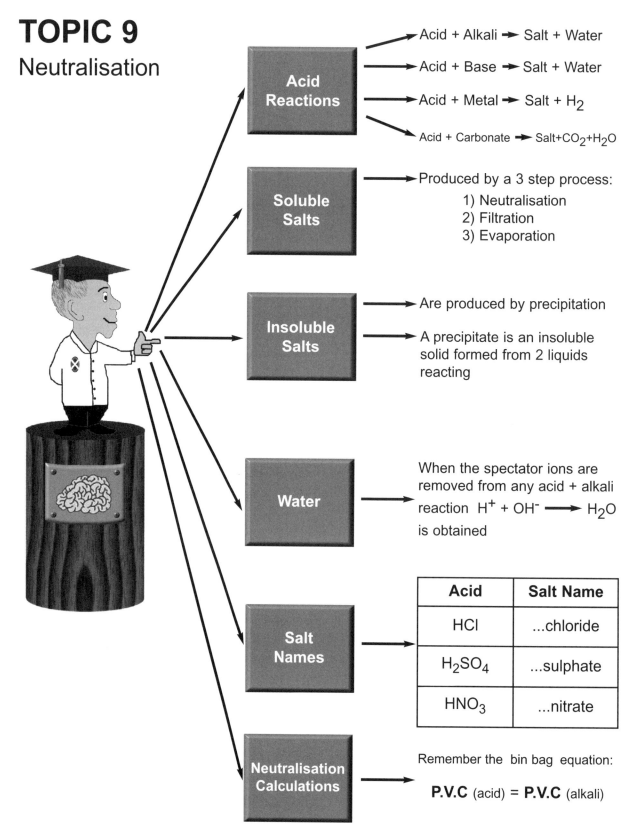

Acid Reactions

- Acid + Alkali → Salt + Water
- Acid + Base → Salt + Water
- Acid + Metal → Salt + H_2
- Acid + Carbonate → Salt + CO_2 + H_2O

Soluble Salts

Produced by a 3 step process:
1) Neutralisation
2) Filtration
3) Evaporation

Insoluble Salts

Are produced by precipitation

A precipitate is an insoluble solid formed from 2 liquids reacting

Water

When the spectator ions are removed from any acid + alkali reaction $H^+ + OH^- \longrightarrow H_2O$ is obtained

Salt Names

Acid	Salt Name
HCl	...chloride
H_2SO_4	...sulphate
HNO_3	...nitrate

Neutralisation Calculations

Remember the bin bag equation:

P.V.C (acid) = **P.V.C** (alkali)

TOPIC 10
Making Electricity

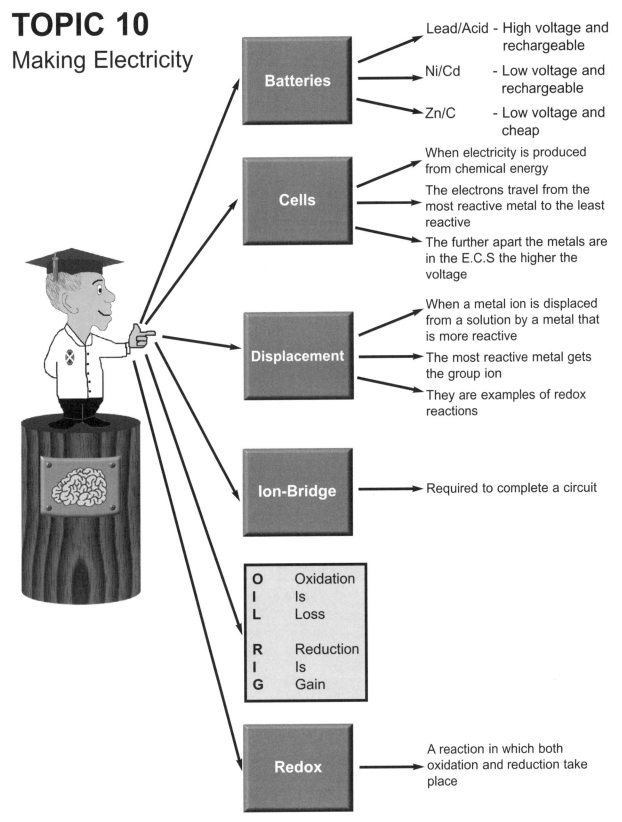

Batteries
- Lead/Acid - High voltage and rechargeable
- Ni/Cd - Low voltage and rechargeable
- Zn/C - Low voltage and cheap

Cells
- When electricity is produced from chemical energy
- The electrons travel from the most reactive metal to the least reactive
- The further apart the metals are in the E.C.S the higher the voltage

Displacement
- When a metal ion is displaced from a solution by a metal that is more reactive
- The most reactive metal gets the group ion
- They are examples of redox reactions

Ion-Bridge
- Required to complete a circuit

O	Oxidation
I	Is
L	Loss
R	Reduction
I	Is
G	Gain

Redox
- A reaction in which both oxidation and reduction take place

TOPIC 11
Metals

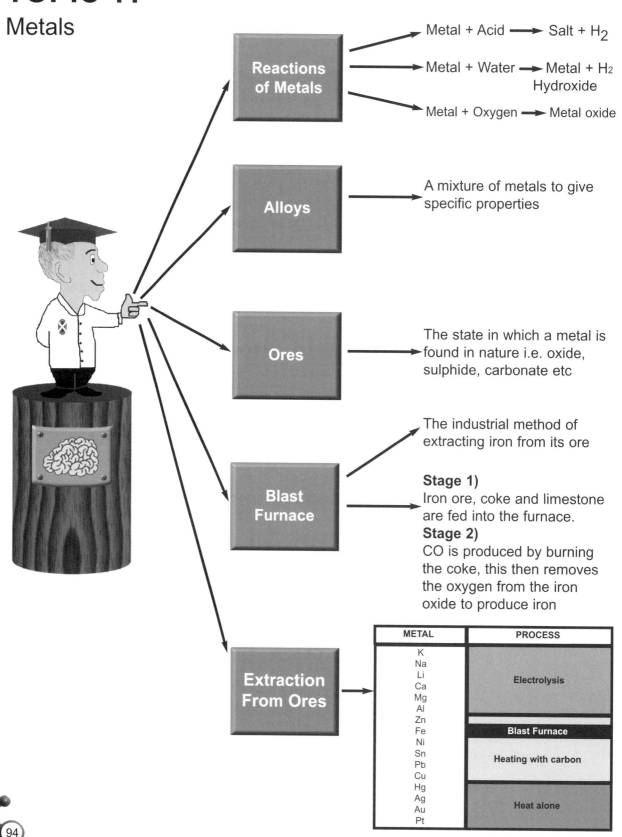

Reactions of Metals

Metal + Acid → Salt + H_2

Metal + Water → Metal + H_2
Hydroxide

Metal + Oxygen → Metal oxide

Alloys

A mixture of metals to give specific properties

Ores

The state in which a metal is found in nature i.e. oxide, sulphide, carbonate etc

Blast Furnace

The industrial method of extracting iron from its ore

Stage 1)
Iron ore, coke and limestone are fed into the furnace.
Stage 2)
CO is produced by burning the coke, this then removes the oxygen from the iron oxide to produce iron

Extraction From Ores

METAL	PROCESS
K
Na
Li
Ca
Mg
Al
Zn	Electrolysis
Fe	Blast Furnace
Ni
Sn
Pb
Cu	Heating with carbon
Hg
Ag
Au
Pt	Heat alone

TOPIC 12
Corrosion

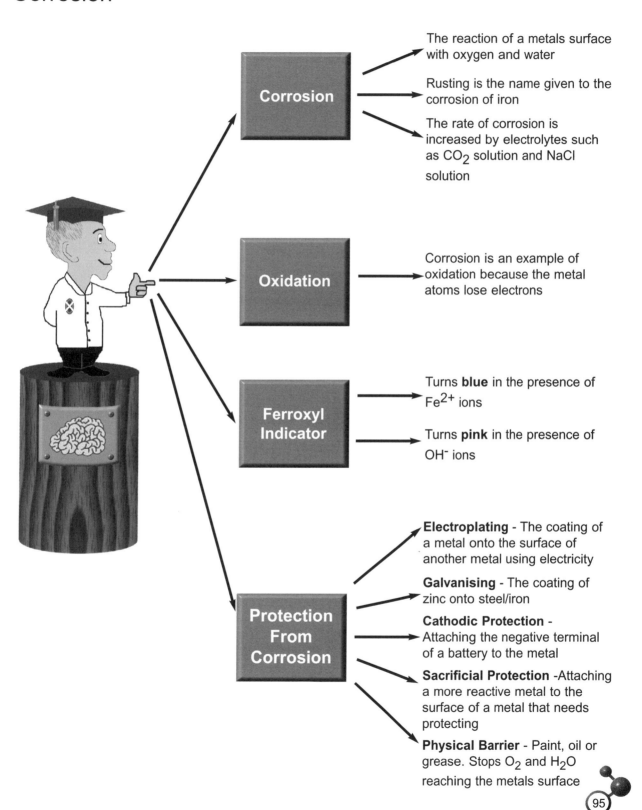

Corrosion
- The reaction of a metals surface with oxygen and water
- Rusting is the name given to the corrosion of iron
- The rate of corrosion is increased by electrolytes such as CO_2 solution and NaCl solution

Oxidation
- Corrosion is an example of oxidation because the metal atoms lose electrons

Ferroxyl Indicator
- Turns **blue** in the presence of Fe^{2+} ions
- Turns **pink** in the presence of OH^- ions

Protection From Corrosion
- **Electroplating** - The coating of a metal onto the surface of another metal using electricity
- **Galvanising** - The coating of zinc onto steel/iron
- **Cathodic Protection** - Attaching the negative terminal of a battery to the metal
- **Sacrificial Protection** -Attaching a more reactive metal to the surface of a metal that needs protecting
- **Physical Barrier** - Paint, oil or grease. Stops O_2 and H_2O reaching the metals surface

95

TOPIC 13
Plastics

Plastics → Synthetic materials made from crude oil

Pollution →
- Most plastics are non-biodegradable
- **HCl** - a corrosive gas produced when PVC burns
- **HCN** - a toxic gas produced when polyurethane is burned
- **CO** - a toxic gas produced on combustion of any plastic

Monomers → Small molecules that combine to form one large polymer molecule

Polymer → The very large molecules produced when many monomers combine

Addition Polymerisation → The process in which many **unsaturated** monomers combine across their double bonds to form a polymer. See page 69 & 70

Repeating Unit → A short hand drawing of a polymer chain. Shown below is the repeating unit of polypropene

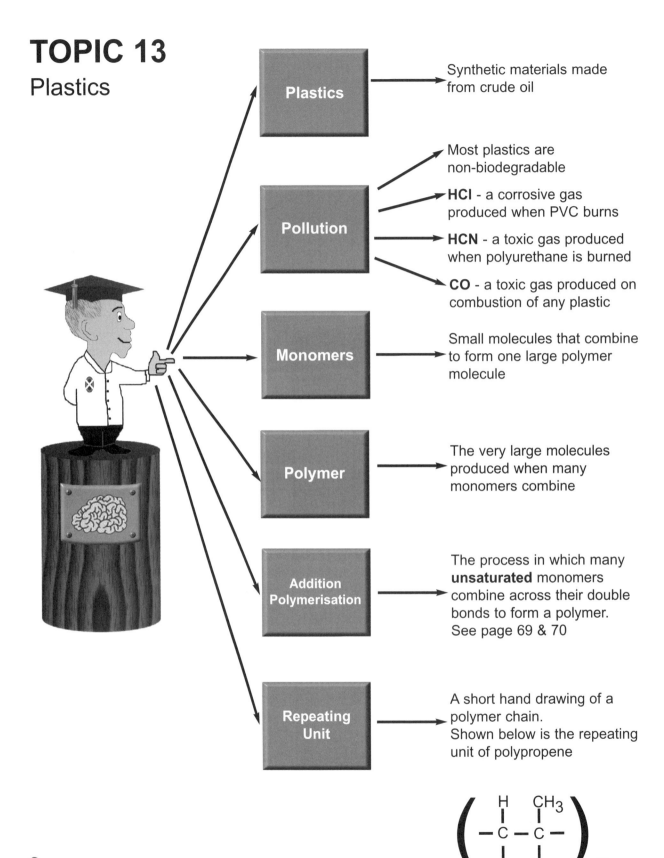

TOPIC 14
Fertilisers

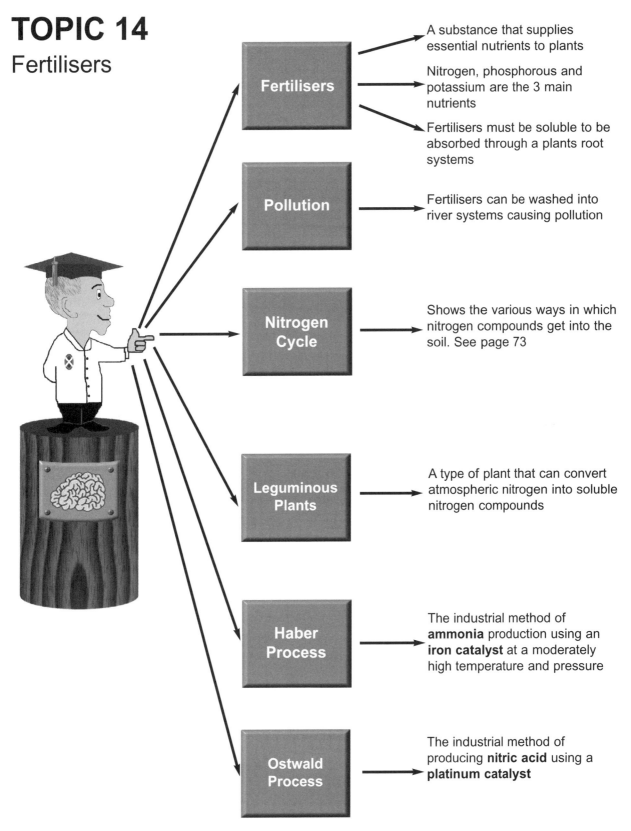

Fertilisers
- A substance that supplies essential nutrients to plants
- Nitrogen, phosphorous and potassium are the 3 main nutrients
- Fertilisers must be soluble to be absorbed through a plants root systems

Pollution
- Fertilisers can be washed into river systems causing pollution

Nitrogen Cycle
- Shows the various ways in which nitrogen compounds get into the soil. See page 73

Leguminous Plants
- A type of plant that can convert atmospheric nitrogen into soluble nitrogen compounds

Haber Process
- The industrial method of **ammonia** production using an **iron catalyst** at a moderately high temperature and pressure

Ostwald Process
- The industrial method of producing **nitric acid** using a **platinum catalyst**

TOPIC 15
Carbohydrates

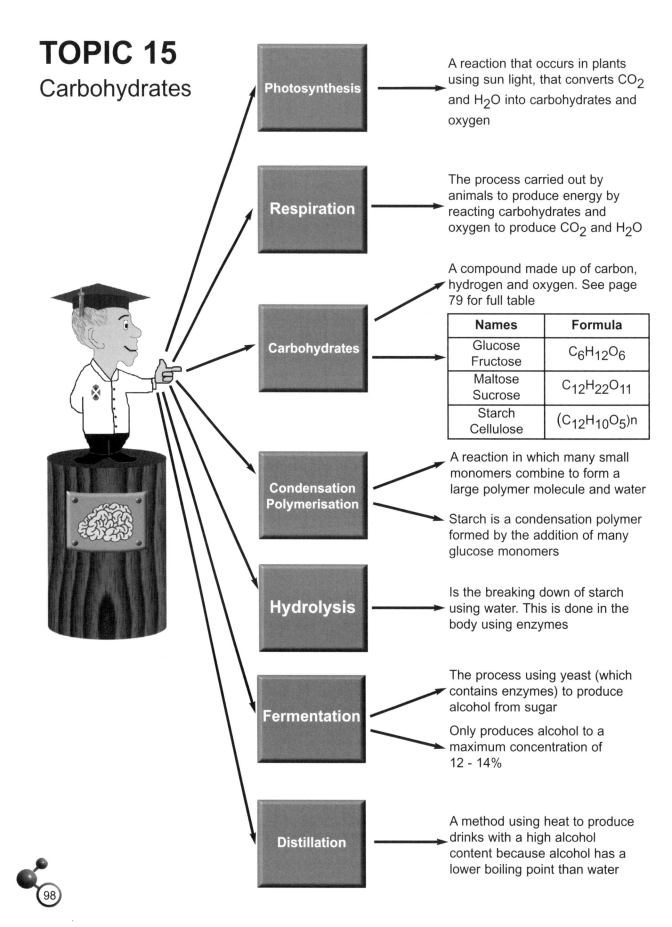

Photosynthesis → A reaction that occurs in plants using sun light, that converts CO_2 and H_2O into carbohydrates and oxygen

Respiration → The process carried out by animals to produce energy by reacting carbohydrates and oxygen to produce CO_2 and H_2O

Carbohydrates → A compound made up of carbon, hydrogen and oxygen. See page 79 for full table

Names	Formula
Glucose Fructose	$C_6H_{12}O_6$
Maltose Sucrose	$C_{12}H_{22}O_{11}$
Starch Cellulose	$(C_{12}H_{10}O_5)n$

Condensation Polymerisation → A reaction in which many small monomers combine to form a large polymer molecule and water

→ Starch is a condensation polymer formed by the addition of many glucose monomers

Hydrolysis → Is the breaking down of starch using water. This is done in the body using enzymes

Fermentation → The process using yeast (which contains enzymes) to produce alcohol from sugar

→ Only produces alcohol to a maximum concentration of 12 - 14%

Distillation → A method using heat to produce drinks with a high alcohol content because alcohol has a lower boiling point than water

Essential Equations

Metal + Oxygen $\longrightarrow$ Metal oxide

Metal + Water $\longrightarrow$ Metal + Hydrogen Hydroxide

Metal + Acid $\longrightarrow$ Salt + Hydrogen

Acid + Alkali $\longrightarrow$ Salt + Water

Acid + Base $\longrightarrow$ Salt + Water

Metal + Acid carbonate $\longrightarrow$ Salt + H_2O + CO_2

Carbon + Oxygen $\longrightarrow$ Carbon dioxide

Hydrogen + Oxygen $\longrightarrow$ Water

Hydrocarbon + Oxygen $\longrightarrow$ CO_2 + H_2O

REMEMBER
The reaction may or may not take place, it depends on the reactivity of the metals or the concentration of the reactants.

Chemical Dictionary

Acid — A substance with a pH below 7 because it has a higher concentration of H^+ ions than water. (Page 42)

Acid Rain — A form of pollution caused by gases such as SO_2 and NO_2 which dissolve in rain water lowering the pH of the rain water below 7. (Page 27/41)

Addition Polymerisation — A reaction in which many small monomers combine to form one large polymer molecule. (Page 70)

Addition Reaction — A reaction in which a small molecule usually a diatomic molecule adds across the double bond of an alkene. (Page 33)

Alkali — A substance with a pH above 7 because it has a higher concentration of OH^- ions than pure water. (Page 43)

Alkali Metals — The very reactive group 1 metals. (Page 9)

Alkanes — The simplest homologous series of saturated hydrocarbons with the general formula C_nH_{2n+2} (Page 29)

Alkenes — A homologous series of hydrocarbons that are unsaturated and have the general formula C_nH_{2n}. They are isomers of the cylcoalkanes. (Page 31)

Alloy — A mixture of metals mixed to give desired properties. (Page 63)

Atom — A particle made up of protons, neutrons, and electrons. (Page 10)

Atomic Number — The number given to each element in the periodic table. It is equal to the number of protons in an atom. (Page 11)

Base — A substance which neutralises an acid. (Page 43)

Benedicts Reagent — A solution that turns from blue to orange when heated with glucose, fructose and maltose. (Page 79)

Biodegradable — A substance that can rot away naturally. (Page 68)

Blast Furnace — The method in which iron is extracted from its ore. (Page 62)

Carbohydrates — A chemical group that contains carbon, hydrogen and oxygen and provide energy for the body. (Page 77)

Catalyst — Alters the rate of a reaction but is not used up in the reaction. (Page 7)

Catalytic Converter — Part of the exhaust system of a car that converts harmful gases into less harmful gases using a catalyst. (Page 28)

Catalytic Cracking	The breaking up of long chain hydrocarbons into smaller more profitable molecules. (Page 34)
Cathodic Protection	A method of protection from corrosion by attaching the metal to the negative terminal of a battery. (Page 66)
Cell	When electrical energy is produced from chemical energy. (Page 55)
Chromatography	A separation technique that separates a small mixture of liquids. (Page 5)
Compound	A substance made up of 2 or more elements chemically joined. (Page 3)
Concentrated	A solution with a lot of solute dissolved in a little solvent. (Page 4)
Condensation Polymerisation	A type of polymerisation that produces a polymer and water. Starch is a polymeristion condensation polymer. (Page 80)
Corrosion	When the surface of a metal reacts with water and oxygen to form a compound. (Page 64)
Covalent bond	A shared pair of electrons between two non-metals. (Page 15)
Covalent Network	A giant network of atoms held together by covalent bonds they have very high melting and boiling points. (Page 40)
Cycloalkanes	A homologous series with a ring of carbon atoms. They have the general formula of C_nH_{2n}. They are isomers of the alkenes. (Page 32)
Density	The mass of a substance in a given volume. (Page 59)
Diatomic Elements	Elements whose molecules contain two atoms e.g. O_2. Remember the poem... (Page 17)
Dilute solution	A solution with a little solute dissolved in a lot of solvent. (Page 4)
Displacement Reaction	When a metal ion is displaced from a solution by a metal that is higher in the reactivity series. (Page 57)
Distillation	A separation technique that separates a mixture of liquids with different boiling points. (Page 82)
Electrolysis	The separation of an ionic solution using a D.C. power supply. (Page 37/44)
Electrolyte	An ionic solution which conducts electricity. (Page 37)
Electron	A negatively charged particle that has a mass of approx 0. (Page 10)
Electroplating	The coating of a metal onto the surface of another metal using electricity. (Page 66)
Element	Contains only one type of atom. (Page 2)
Empirical Formula	Shows the simplest formula of a compound. (Page 63)

Endothermic A reaction which takes in energy. This means that the temperature usually drops. (Page 2)

Enzyme A biological catalyst. They work well under certain conditions i.e. temperatures and pH (Page 8)

Evaporation Is the process in which a liquid is turned into a gas by heat. It can also be used as a separation technique. (Page 5)

Exothermic A reaction that gives out energy. This results in a temperature increase. (Page 2)

Fermentation The process using yeast that turns sugar and water into alcohol and carbon dioxide. (Page 82)

Ferroxyl Indicator An indicator that turns blue in the presence of Fe^{2+} ions and turns pink in the presence of OH^- ions. (Page 65)

Filtrate The liquid that passes through the filter paper and is collected after filtration. (Page 5)

Filtration A separation technique that separates an insoluble solid from a liquid. (Page 5)

Formula mass The mass of one mole of a substance. (Page 45)

Fossil Fuels Coal,Oil and Gas. They were formed by dead plants and animals kept under pressure for millions of years. (Page 24)

Fraction A group of compounds within a narrow range of boiling points produced from fractional distillation. (Page 25)

Fractional Distillation A technique used to separate crude oil into fractions with similar boiling points using heat. (Page 25)

Fuel A substance that reacts exothermically with oxygen. (Page 22)

Galvanising The coating of iron with zinc. (Page 66)

Haber Process The industrial method of ammonia production using an iron catalyst. (Page 74)

Halogens The reactive non-metals in group 7 of the periodic table. (Page 9)

Homologous Series A family of compounds with similar chemical properties that can be represented by a general formula. (Page 29)

Hydrocarbon A compound made up of carbon and hydrogen. (Page 25)

Ion A charged particle formed by the losing (metals) or gaining (non-metals) of electrons. (Page 37)

Ion Bridge Used to complete the circuit in a cell. (Page 56)

Ionic Bond	The electrostatic force of attraction between a positive metal ion and a negative non-metal ion. (Page 36)
Ionic Lattice	A large arrangement of ions held together by ionic bonds. They have high melting and boiling points and dissolve in water. They conduct when molten or in solution. (Page 39)
Isomers	Compounds with the same molecular formula but a different structural formula. (Page 33)
Isotope	Atoms with the same atomic number but different mass numbers. (Page 14)
Leguminous Plant	A type of plant that can covert atmospheric nitrogen into nitrogen compounds that they use to provide nutrients. (Page 72)
Malleable	The ability of a metal to be rolled or beaten into thin sheets. (Page 59)
Mass Number	Equal to the number of protons plus neutrons in an atom. (Page 13)
Mixture	Two or more substances mixed but not chemically joined. (Page 4)
Mole	The formula mass of a substance. (Page 45)
Molecule	Two or more atoms held together by covalent bonds. (Page 15)
Monomer	Small molecules that combine to form a large polymer molecule. (Page 69)
Neutralisation	The reaction of an acid with an alkali or a base that moves the pH towards 7. (Page 48)
Neutron	A particle in an atom which is found in the nucleus and has a mass of 1. (Page 10)
Noble Gas	Very unreactive non-metals found in group 8 of the periodic table. (Page 9)
Nucleus	The positively charged centre of an atom that contains the neutrons and protons. (Page 10)
Ore	The state in which a metal is found in nature. (Page 61)
Ostwald Process	The industrial method of production nitric acid from ammonia using a platinum catalyst. (Page 75)
Oxidation Reaction	A reaction in which electrons are lost. (Page 58)
pH	A number that indicates the acidity and alkalinity of a substance. (Page 42)
Photosynthesis	The process carried out by plants using sunlight that converts carbon dioxide and water into carbohydrates and oxygen. (Page 77)
Polymer	A very large molecule formed by the addition of many small monomer molecules. (Page 69)

Polymerisation The reaction in which a polymer is formed. (Page 69)

Precipitate An insoluble substance formed by the reaction of two liquids. (Page 51)

Proton A small positively charged particle found in the nucleus of an atom. It has a mass of 1. (Page 10)

Reactivity Series A list of metals (and hydrogen) in order of reactivity. (Page 53)

Redox Reaction A reaction in which both oxidation and reduction take place. (Page 58)

Reduction Reaction A reaction in which electrons are gained. (Page 58)

Relative Atomic Mass The average mass of all the isotopes of an element. (Page 14)

Residue The insoluble solid left over in the filter paper after filtration. (Page 5)

Respiration The reaction of oxygen with food inside the body to provide energy and also produces water and carbon dioxide. (Page 78)

Rusting The corrosion of iron. (Page 64)

Sacrificial Protection A method of protecting a metal from corrosion by connecting it to a more reactive metal. (Page 67)

Salt A product of neutralization. In which the hydrogen ion of an acid has been replaced by the ammonium ion or metal ion of the alkali. (Page 48)

Saturated Hydrocarbon A hydrocarbon that has only single carbon to carbon bonds (alkanes and cycloalkanes). (Page 32)

Saturated Solution A solution in which no more solute can dissolve. (Page 4)

Solute The substance that dissolves in the solvent. (Page 4)

Solvent The liquid in the which the solute dissolves. (Page 4)

Spectator ion Ion that is present during a reaction but remains unchanged by the reaction. (Page 51)

Standard Solution A solution which has a known and accurately measured concentration. (Page 52)

Thermoplastic A plastic that will soften on heating and can be reshaped. (Page 69)

Thermosetting Plastic — A plastic that doesn't soften on heating. (Page 69)

Unsaturated Hydrocarbon — A hydrocarbon that contains at least one carbon to carbon double bond such as Alkenes. (Page 32)

Valency — The number of bonds that an element or group ion can form. (Page 18)

Viscosity — The measure of how thick or runny a substance is. (Page 26)

Word Equation — An equation in which the names of the reactants and products are shown rather than chemical symbols and formulas.